Thomas Balguy

Divine Benevolence Asserted and Vindicated from the Objections of Ancient and Modern Sceptics

Thomas Balguy

Divine Benevolence Asserted and Vindicated from the Objections of Ancient and Modern Sceptics

ISBN/EAN: 9783337779832

Printed in Europe, USA, Canada, Australia, Japan

Cover: Foto ©Lupo / pixelio.de

More available books at **www.hansebooks.com**

DIVINE BENEVOLENCE

ASSERTED;

AND VINDICATED FROM

THE OBJECTIONS

OF

ANCIENT AND MODERN SCEPTICS.

By THOMAS BALGUY, D.D.

ARCHDEACON OF WINCHESTER.

Faciam rem non difficilem, caufam Deorum agam.
SEN. de Prov.

LONDON:

Printed for LOCKYER DAVIS, in Holbourn,
Printer to the Royal Society.

M.DCC.LXXXI.

ADVERTISEMENT.

THE following Treatise is a specimen of a larger work on the subject of natural religion: why published at this time, will be too easily conjectured.

This subject is reducible to three general heads: God's being, his perfection, his moral government.

I. To prove the *being* of God, is to prove the existence of a wise and benevolent Author of Nature. The name of GOD would be improperly applied, either to an *unconcerned* spectator of natural events, or an *undiscerning* cause, or a *malevolent* author, and contriver, of them. The idea therefore signified by this name, includes the three attributes of *power*, *wisdom*, and *goodness*.

Power and wisdom will appear in a most amazing degree, if *each* part of the universe
proceed

proceed from an *intelligent* cause, and *all* its parts from *one* and the *same* cause.—Goodness is the subject of the following papers.

II. To prove the *perfection* of God, is to prove that he unites in himself every *kind* and *degree* of these attributes, which really *exists* in the universe; and this, without any limitation of *time* or *place*.

I say not, that he possesses all *conceivable* power, &c. for we are very apt to *misconceive*. I *need* not say, that he possesses *infinite* power, &c. for this expression has no other meaning than what has already been pointed out.

III. On the subject of God's *moral government*, it ought to be shewn,

1. That men are *actually* under divine government.

2. That the laws of this government are *moral*.

3. That the laws are *imperfectly* executed.

4. That the seeming defects and errors of God's *present* government will be supplied and corrected in a *future state*.

On the *last* of these heads God has not seen fit to give us that full and decisive evidence, which our fond imaginations might lead us to expect. *Nature* indeed suggests the *hopes* of future happiness. But it was reserved for the *Christian revelation* to bring *life and immortality to light*.

The best *foundation* for such hopes, as may be derived from *natural* appearances, would be laid in the following propositions:

1st. That men will continue to *exist* after death, and will continue *subject* to God's *moral government*.

2dly. That their present and future existence are parts of *one scheme*.

3dly. That this scheme will either continually *approach* to perfection, or become, in time, *absolutely perfect*.

From this sketch the reader will understand, that the reflections laid before him, however imperfect, are no hasty production; but the result of care and thought. Possibly the outlines here drawn will, at some time or other, be filled up.

CONTENTS.

Part the First.

Introduction, p. 5.

Sect. I. Of the bodies of men and other animals; in reference to
  1. Preservation and destruction, p. 18.
  2. Sense and motion, p. 27.

Sect. II. Of the external and inanimate causes, which are capable of affecting animal bodies: viz. the causes of
  1. Preservation and pleasure, p. 30.
  2. Destruction and pain, p. 37.

Recapitulation, p. 39.

Sect. III. Of the human mind.—viz. 1. The understanding, p. 41. 2. The will, p. 44.

3. The passions, viz. p. 47.
  1st. Selfish, or those which regard ourselves, p. 49.
  2dly. Social and malevolent, which regard others, p. 53.
  3dly. Moral, which regard both ourselves and others, p. 61.

Remarks taken from Hutcheson, p. 75.

Sect. IV. On the mutual dependence of men and other animals, p. 77.

Sect. V. On the mutual dependence of mankind, p. 79.

Objections

CONTENTS.

Objections considered in

Sect. I. { On the means of preservation, p. 21.
On the means of destruction. { Obj. 1. p. 24.
Obj. 2. ib.
Obj. 3. p. 25.
Obj. 4. p. 26. }

Sect. II. Of the causes of preservation and pleasure. { Obj. 1. p. 31.
Obj. 2. p. 33.
Obj. 3. p. 36. }

Sect. III. { Of the will, p. 45.
Of the passions, viz. objections against { particular passions, p. 59.
all the passions. { 1. p. 64.
2. ib. } }

General objection to the constitution of human nature, p. 67.

Sect. IV. Of the mutual dependence of men and other animals, p. 78.

Sect. V. Of the mutual dependence of mankind, p. 80.

Part the Second.

I. Of the more general laws of divine administration, p. 82.

1. That the happiness of men is made to depend on their actions, p. 83.

2. That they are excited to perform these actions by punishments, as well as rewards, p. 87.

3. That, in both ways, they are excited to hurtful, as well as beneficial, actions, p. 90.

II. Of the uniformity, with which God's laws are administered, p. 91.

III. Of

III. Of the oppofition made by human agents to the ends of divine government, p. 97.

Part the Third.

Introduction, p. 103.

I. Circumftances pointed out, which may incline us to admit the doctrine of prepollent good: refpecting
- 1. Ourfelves, p. 106.
- 2. Thofe we know, p. 107.
- 3. Thofe we do not know, p. 108.

II. Objections to this doctrine
- 1. Even in peaceful times; refpecting thofe who are
  - fuccefsful, p. 111.
  - unfuccefsful, p. 115.
- 2. Drawn from war and it's confequences, p. 117.
- 3. The cafes of tyranny and perfecution, p. 120.
- 4. The chief events recorded in hiftory, p. 122.

Appendix, p. 127.

DIVINE BENEVOLENCE

ASSERTED, &c.

THE divine goodness is considered by some writers as consisting wholly in *benevolence*: by others, as comprehending some other moral perfections, not perhaps reducible to this head. But the idea of benevolence is by all writers *included* under that of goodness; and is at least a very affecting and interesting part of it: and this only is the subject of the following disquisition.

That the Author of Nature has been influenced by a benevolent principle, both in framing and preserving the universe, is usually proved from the degree of happiness *actually* produced in this system; or at least from the *prepollency* of good. But this argument alone may not perhaps give intire satisfaction

faction to a scrupulous inquirer. If we consider the good *only*, exclusively of the evil, our premises will be too narrow to support our conclusion. If we consider *both*, we may more easily satisfy ourselves, than prove to the conviction of others, that the good exceeds the evil.

There are indeed writers of great authority, who think we may *demonstrate* the goodness of our Creator from the marks and effects of goodness discernible in his works. When this is once done, we need not, they say, pay any regard to contrary appearances; for that difficulties are not to be urged against demonstration.—Certainly they are not. But in the present case, it is to be feared, the term is misapplied. For we shall not be justified, on any sound principles of logic, in drawing an universal conclusion from a partial and imperfect view. The intention of our Maker is to be collected from the *whole* system of nature; so far at least as falls within our observation: not from detached parts of it. We have no right therefore to form any judgment about it, till the *evils*, as well as the *goods*, of life, have been fully considered.

The other method of arguing, viz. from the *prepollency* of good, stands indeed on a wider, but not perhaps a surer, bottom. It is difficult for a man to estimate any *single* pleasure or pain, felt by another man: still more difficult to compute the *sum* of his pleasures or pains, and then to balance the account. How then shall we be able to estimate the clear amount, whether of happiness or misery, among the whole race of mankind; especially if it be considered, how very small a part of our species falls directly under our observation?

It may be more satisfactory then to consider separately the various *causes* of pleasure and pain: and to examine how far these opposite *effects* were *designed* or *accidental*; i. e. whether either or both were *ultimate ends**. If the constitution and laws of *every* part of nature appear ultimately intended to produce good; it cannot but be the joint intention of *all* the parts. Nor shall we have any suffi-

---

* By the word *ultimate* we only mean the last *discernible* intention. Our present state *may* have reference to other states and other systems. But this being unknown, proves nothing for, or against, the divine goodness.

cient reason to reject this conclusion, if *many* of the phænomena, not all, shew an intention of producing good: and *no* part, or circumstance, shew an intention of producing evil except only in *subordination* to good; which, to the purpose of our present inquiry, is in truth no exception at all.

Not only we may discover the intention of nature by contemplating the several *parts* of the universe, and the *respective* laws to which each of them is subject: but the more *general* laws, which extend through God's *whole* administration, may with great probability be urged as proofs of good or of evil intention.—Even the propriety of governing *at all* by fixed and settled laws, is a very material subject of inquiry: and it may also seem to many both a doubtful and an important question, how far it is conceivable, that a benevolent author of nature should permit the good effect of these laws to be *opposed* and *defeated* by the folly and perverseness of human agents. When these inquiries are finished, we shall then come with advantage consider the actual *result* of the various ies of divine administration.

PART

PART I.

INTRODUCTION.

THE same observations, which shew, that the phænomena of nature are produced with design, usually determine in each particular case *what* that design was. But, the particular effects being innumerable, the immediate ends of them must be also innumerable. These effects however being many of them similar, the ends proposed must be also similar. These ends then, as well as the phænomena themselves, are capable of being reduced under certain *general heads:* that is, they may be distributed into various *classes*, like effects, or like ends, being thrown into the same class. It is thus we determine the *laws* which direct the constitution of nature, as well as the *views* with which it is so constituted and governed.

As a great number of these general *laws* may often be resolved into one still *more* general; so a number of *designs* may be also referred to a yet *higher* design, in which they are all included: and it is the business of philosophers to reduce both to as few and as simple principles as they can.

We are first then to reduce the various intentions discernible in the constitution and course of nature to a few general principles; and then to comprehend these, if that appear to be possible, under one *more* general and simple principle.

Now the various intentions discernible in the works of Nature, are all reducible to these two;

1. To produce a regular succession of men and animals; including the birth, temporary preservation, decay, and dissolution of each individual.

2. To furnish them with the means and occasions of exercising their various powers of perception and action.

It will appear from a very slight induction, that these intentions concur in the various works of nature; and it will also appear; that the first is subordinate to the second.

PARTICULARS

Particulars.

1. Very many *vegetables* are relative to these purposes; being designed in part for the subsistence of men and animals, and in part for the various uses of life.

2. *Fossils* and *minerals* were designed for the use of man*.

3. *Springs* and *rivers* are designed for the subsistence and use both of men and animals; for promoting also the fertility of the earth, i. e. the production of vegetables; and in this way also for the service of men and animals.

4. The *earth* was designed for an habitation to men and animals: also for the production of fossils, minerals, vegetables.

5. The *sea* was designed as a habitation for innumerable tribes of fishes; for the production also of vapours, which fall in rain, producing vegetables for the use of men and animals.

6. The *sun* and *moon* are both mediately and immediately necessary for the subsistence and use of animals, and especially of men.

---

* So says Cicero (de Nat. Deor. lib. 11. c. 64) Nec vero supra terram, sed etiam in intimis ejus tenebris plurimarum rerum latet utilitas; quæ, ad usum hominum orta, ab hominibus solis invenitur.

7. The formation of *men* and other *animals* was plainly intended for the temporary production of sense and motion; for continuing these powers during a limited time of uncertain extent; for transmitting them in succession from one individual to another.

With what view now are these several successions of men and animals produced and preserved? Doubtless with a design that they should *live*; *i. e.* perceive and act in various ways. And to what purpose are the several individuals destroyed? Without question, to make way for others, that these also may perceive and act. There may indeed be *other* intentions. But this, *of itself*, will account for all the phænomena. For the design of causing a variety of perceptions and actions, evidently includes and presupposes the design of producing and preserving; and a design of transmitting life to a new race of beings, equally includes the design of removing, if not of destroying, those which already exist on the same globe.—*Perception* then and *action*, in various kinds, include all the known intentions of the Author of Nature.—But this

this perhaps may require farther illustration. Let us then consider the subject a little more particularly.

1. An animal body is a machine endued with various powers of sense and motion; and many of the parts of which it consists (perhaps all of them) are subservient either to the *existence* of these powers, or to the *use* of them.

2. It is a general law of the animal creation, that these powers must be *exercised* in order to their preservation: not only because they are strengthened by a proper use of them, but because, if we should neglect to use them, life itself could not be sustained; the motive powers being evidently necessary for obtaining those gratifications of sense, which are the means of supporting the whole machine, and so of continuing the powers thus employed.

3. But, as Nature has provided for the employment of these powers with a view to their continuance, so also for their continuance with a view to their actual employment.

4. Yet it would be absurd to suppose that these ends are reciprocal. To say we exist merely

merely for the sake of perception and action, yet perceive and act for the sake of continuing our existence, is to say, that the animal machine is formed for no purpose at all. One of these ends must be *principally* intended; the other purely *subordinate*.

5. It would be absurd to suppose that the end principally intended is preservation; and that perception and action are subordinate to it: for this is only to say, that these effects are constantly produced, for the sake of making it *possible*, that they should be *repeated*. Whereas, if the *actual* repetition of them be indifferent, the possibility of repetition can be no purpose at all.

6. The powers however of sense and motion may both be considered as occasions of our preservation, and also as occasions of our pleasures and pains; and the pleasures and pains resulting from them either as *subordinate* to our preservation, or as being themselves the *principal* ends, for the sake of which we are produced and preserved. For there is no absurdity in supposing, that the very same sensations, which were principally intended, should also be made subordinate to

our

our preservation, and so become the occasions of reproducing themselves.

In consequence of these remarks we may now set aside the first of those general intentions, which were above pointed out, and consider *perception* and *action* as the *sole* ends (within the compass of human reason) proposed by the Author of Nature.

But we may advance one step farther than this. For the actions of men and other animals are the *causes* of perception to the agent and to others; and are frequently also the causes of production, preservation, and destruction. These then are to be considered as *subordinate* to perception, which we may fairly conclude to be the ultimate end in the contemplation of our Maker.

The only question remaining is, What *kind* of perception was intended by the Author of Nature, whether pleasant, or painful, or both.

Now the fact is, that men, and all other animals, have perception of *both* kinds; and from the frame of their nature, and the circumstances in which they are placed, such perceptions must have been foreseen. But, consistently confiftently with this fact, and the foreknowledge of it, three fuppofitions may be made.

1. That the pleafures and pains, arifing from the conftitution of Nature, were *equally* intended by its author: *i.e.* he was induced to make things, as they are, by *both* motives; or both pleafure and pain were *ultimate ends*. On this fuppofition God is a *capricious* being.

2. That the *pleafures only* were intended; and that the pains are accidental confequences attending the means of producing pleafure: *i.e.* the pains arifing in the prefent fyftem of things are *not* ultimate ends; but unhappy appendages of a fcheme formed with no other defign then the production of good. On this fuppofition, God is a *benevolent* being.—Or

3. That the *pains only* were intended; the pleafures being nothing more than accidental confequences of the means ufed for caufing pain: *i.e.* the pleafures are not ultimate ends, but neceffary parts of a fcheme defigned purely for the production of evil. On this fuppofition God is a *malevolent* being.

Now, previous to a particular enquiry, we may point out perhaps fome circumftances, which

which will form a strong presumptive proof in favour of the *second* of these suppositions.

1. It is more probable that God is *good* than *capricious*; because the course of nature is *uniform*. Whatever events befall us, good or bad, arise from certain *general* principles in the constitution and government of the universe. Now, from the nature of a world so framed, and a government so conducted, many events would be likely to happen, contrary to the intention of its Author. But it is *not* likely, that a capricious Being should be constant and uniform in his methods of acting; when the ends of his administration would be at least equally well answered by variety and disorder.

2. It is more probable, that God is *good* than *evil*. For evil, as far as we can judge, is more likely to be *accidental*. This appears from experience in the conduct of men; who usually act with a design of producing good either to themselves or to others. The evil they do is often indeed foreseen, but seldom desired or pursued as the ultimate end of action. This analogy is not to be slighted. Whoever admits the usual proofs of a signed-

designing cause of the universe, must allow us to argue, so we do it with proper caution, from *human* designs to *divine*. But there is still something more in the case here. For the production of good requires *uniform* conduct: and he who acts by rule will of course sometimes produce effects *not intended*. The intention therefore of producing good may, by accident, occasion evil. But the *contrary* intention will scarce ever occasion good: because evil, for the most part, may easily be produced, without observing any rule at all; and often the *more* easily on that very account.—Add to this, that a good design is in every view more *difficult* to be executed, than an evil one; and therefore is more likely to be executed *imperfectly*: i. e. with a mixture of effects foreign to the design or opposite to it*. It

---

* When these papers were first drawn up, it was believed, that the three suppositions above-mentioned were the only suppositions which could possibly be made by one who admits the unity of God. But a late writer has invented a fourth, viz. that *neither* our pleasure nor pains were ultimately intended by the Author of Nature. He is supposed to be void of benevolence and void of malice.—This is totally repugnant to all the experience we have of the conduct of intelligent beings. Could it be admitted at all, it would, in a great degree, subvert the evidence of a designing cause

It is perhaps needless to observe that all this reasoning presupposes the divine UNITY: a truth, as it seems, easily deducible from the *similitude* of design, and the *unity* of design, which appear in the works of nature. But this subject is not within the compass of our present inquiry.

We may now therefore proceed more directly and particularly to examine and lay open the subject before us—viz.

Whether the several parts of the universe, and the laws to which they are subject, were designed by the author of them for the production of Good. In other words, whether the successive existence, perceptions, and actions, of the various animals which inhabit the globe, and the causes on which they depend, all of them proceeding from the *intention* of their maker, be reducible to a *higher*,

cause at the head of the universe; a conclusion, which rests on this principle, that *usefulness* is a mark of design.—It is true, indeed, that men, in most of their designs, mean only to be useful to *themselves:* and, in some of them, aim at *mischief* to others. But *all* their designs have a view to the *feelings* of sensible Beings; and we cannot so much as imagine an elaborate scheme to be formed and executed, without even a wish, that any person living should either be the better or the worse for it.

or

or *more general* intention, viz. the production of happiness.

Now, 1. The *birth* and *preservation* of animals *may* be referred to this end, or may, with equal probability, be referred to an opposite end; viz. the production of misery. For neither happiness nor misery can be produced, unless animals *begin* to live and *continue* to live. The judgement therefore to be formed on this part of the constitution of things depend on the *state* and *condition* allotted to sensible Beings in the present system. If they are intended for a happy state, their production and preservation were instances of goodness; if for a miserable state were instances of malevolence. Birth and Preservation are neither good nor evil.—In like manner

2. The *death* of animals is, *of itself*, neither good nor evil: not to the individual, unless you previously determine, whether its life were happy or miserable; not to the species on *any* supposition. For there is just as much benevolence in communicating happiness, and as much malevolence in communicating misery, to a *succession* of Beings, as in confining

confining it perpetually to the *same* Beings. What one loses, another gains.

To judge then of the general principle; which includes all the ends discernible in the constitution of things, we must consider the nature and condition of men and other animals, during their abode on this globe: i. e. whether their frame and circumstances be adapted to make them happy or miserable. —In the pursuit of this inquiry it will be fit to consider, 1. The constitution of the bodies of animals: 2. The external causes which are capable of affecting them: 3. The powers and faculties of the human mind: 4. The mutual dependence of men and other animals. 5. The mutual dependence of mankind.

PREVIOUS REMARK.

An intention of producing good will be sufficiently apparent in any particular instance, if the thing considered can neither be changed nor taken away, without loss or harm, *all other things continuing the same.* Should you suppose *various* things in the system changed *at once*, you can neither judge of the possibility, nor the consequences, of the change, having no degree of experience to direct you.

This remark is to be carried along through the *whole* proof of divine benevolence.

I.

Of the bodies of men and other animals.

These may be considered in two views: either in reference to preservation and destruction, or to sense and motion.

1. *Of preservation and destruction.*

I. That nature has used fit means for the preservation and succession of animals, is, as we have just seen, no argument of benevolence. The appetites therefore, which are given for that purpose, determine nothing. Whatever end be proposed by the author of nature, Individuals *must* be preserved, and the species continued. On supposition therefore of good, or of ill, design, hunger, thirst, &c. are equally necessary.

II. On the other hand, the *insufficiency* of these means is no argument of malevolence. Thus the frailty of our bodies, which makes them in many ways liable to destruction, and sure of being destroyed in time, will evidently determine nothing in the present question.

For this only shews, that the life of each individual was designed to have *some limit*, and that limit *uncertain*: a design, at least equally consistent with a good or evil principle of action.

But tho' no conclusion can be drawn from the *accomplishment* of these ends, or the *degree* in which they are accomplished; yet the *manner* of doing it may furnish us with some remarks.

III. When we consider the subject in this view, two circumstances especially may seem to deserve our notice.

1st. That all animals are intrusted with the care of preserving *themselves*, and continuing their *species*.

2dly. That we are excited to discharge these offices by reward and punishment.—Thus the neglect of taking sustenance is punished by the sensations of appetite: either neglect or excess is punished by sickness: inattention to danger by external pains. We are often too restrained from the use of improper food by disagreeable sensations.* On the

---

* See Butler's Analogy, Part I.

other hand, all the gratifications of sense within certain limits, may be considered as rewards.

Now the *first* of these circumstances will determine nothing. For it has only these two effects; to make our existence more *precarious*, and to give occasion for the exercise of our *active* faculties. Indeed, *both* circumstances are included under certain general laws, to be considered hereafter, viz. That the happiness of men, and other animals, is made to depend on their *actions*; and that they are obliged to *perform* these actions under the *double* sanction of rewards and punishments.

At present therefore I shall only stay to observe, that the *rewards*, by which we are led to use the means of preservation, &c, are a strong presumption of benevolence. Preservation indeed and succession were equally necessary on either supposition; and the acts, of which we are speaking, are the necessary means, by which those ends are to be obtained. But the pleasures attending them are *not* necessary. The appetites *alone* may seem to have been a sufficient inducement. Whatever pleasure therefore we find in gratifying them, besides the removal of an uneasy sensation, is a good plainly *intended* for us by the Author of Nature. The senses, which produce this pleasure, *could* not have been spared, without lessening our happiness: and *might* have been spared, without discouraging us from preserving ourselves and continuing our species. It is clear, therefore, that the Author of Nature designed, in this instance, to add to our happiness.

Can a similar argument be used to establish the *opposite* conclusion? I think not. But it will be more convenient to defer this subject, till we come to speak of the *more general* laws of divine administration. One objection however occurs, which it may be proper just to touch upon in this place.

Obj. It is alleged, that the uneasy sensation of appetite, in many cases, still continues, after the wants of nature have been supplied; i. e. when it becomes useless or hurtful; and that, on the other hand, agreeable perceptions are often annexed to *excessive* gratification.

Ans. To this objection I shall only answer at present, that we are in no sort competent judges, how far it was *possible* for the palates and stomachs of animals to be differently framed. We complain perhaps of an evil, which admits no remedy; or none but what is worse than the disease.

What more remains to be said on the subject will fall under *another* general law of our nature; viz. That we are often excited to *hurtful*, as well as beneficial, actions.

IV, But as the means of *preservation* furnish no proof of benevolence; so neither do the means of *destruction* furnish any proof of an *opposite* principle. It is only the *manner* in which we are destroyed, on which any argument can be founded. On this head three things are observable; that the time of dying is various and uncertain; that it may be hastened or delayed by the act of the animal itself, or of other animals; and that death is usually preceded by pain and sickness.

1st. The first of these observations affords an instance of benevolence. For the constant foresight of death would render life unhappy*.

2d. The second of them is included in

---

* Οἶμαι δὲ κỳ τὴν φύσιν, ὁρῶσαν τότ' ἄτακλον, κỳ βραχυχρόνιον τῶ βίῳ, ἄδηλον ποιῆσαι τὴν τῶ θανάτω προθεσμίαν, τῶτο γὰρ ἦν ἄμεινον. Εἰ γὰρ προῄδειμεν, κἂν προεξετήκοντό τινες ταῖς λύπαις, κỳ πρὶν ἀποθανεῖν, ἐτεθνήκεισαν. Plut. Conf. ad Apoll.

those

those very general laws, to which we have often occasion to refer, that the happiness of men is made to depend on their actions, and the happiness of one man on the actions of another.

3d. Nor can it be said that the third affords any just presumption of malevolence. For pain and sickness inform us of our danger: prevent us from increasing the mischiefs, which threaten us, by our own misconduct: and often too give room for proper care and fit remedies, by which our lives may be prolonged. This constitution therefore serves to lengthen the time of our existence; and, if our state here be, on the whole, a desireable state, contributes to our good *.

It seems then that the methods used by nature, for preserving and destroying animal bodies, afford some proof of benevolent intention, none of the contrary.—Let us hear, however, what may be urged on the other side.

Now, allowing that pain is useful, by giving us notice of our danger,

---

* Μὴ γὰρ οἰωμεν—οιήσασι δὲ παρῄ τις αἴσθησις ὑπ' ἐν τέμνεσι τι τῶν ἡμετέρων, ὑπ' ἀποσπᾶτο. Τὸ γὰρ ἀκόλιον τοῦτο ἐκ ὄνευ μεγάλων ἐξίεται μισεῖν τὸ ἀνθρώπων. Plat. Ib.

Obj. 1. It may be supposed perhaps, that some *other* kind of notice might have been given, and ought to have been preferred. But this supposition, being wholly imaginary, without any sort of foundation to rest upon, may be safely passed over.

Obj. 2. It may more plausibly be alleged, that the notice is often given, where it must needs prove *ineffectual*. For the uneasy sensations, designed for our preservation, are felt *universally*; even in these instances, where we *cannot* be preserved. But,

1st. How do we know that it was *possible* for the uneasy sensations to be confined and restrained to those particular cases, in which they are capable of producing their full effect? or, if possible, that such restraint would not have been attended with greater loss or harm?

2dly. We may observe, that, as knowlege increases in the world, the number of *remedies* increases, both against outward pains and sickness; and that the pains men suffer, make them more cautious, and more attentive to discover *new* remedies. Fewer instances therefore are likely to occur hereafter, in which these admonitions will prove ineffectual:

fectual: and the time *may* come, when the effect of them will become *constant*; and no species will remain of painful accidents either inevitable or incurable.

5dly. The *general* principle, of annexing pain to the means of destruction, evidently tends to our preservation: and it is this general tendency, of which we now inquire. As to the *constancy* of the laws of nature, in this instance and in others, it will be the subject of a distinct inquiry.

Obj. 3. Though neither the uncertainty of life, nor the penalties by which men and other animals are compelled to preserve it, afford any evidence of malevolence, when taken *separately*; yet taken *together*, they afford a strong proof of malevolent intention. For the frailty of our bodes *continually* exposes us to danger; and therefore we need *frequent* admonitions, i. e. frequent pains. God therefore *intended* that our present condition should be exceedingly liable to pain.— But,

1st. To make this objection conclusive, it must be supposed, that some change could be made in the bodies of animals, wh-

render them *less* frail than they are, without destroying the means of their preservation and happiness; a supposition altogether destitute of proof.

2dly. Though our bodies are made *liable* to pain, yet *actual* pain cannot, with any degree of propriety, be considered as an object of divine intention. For, if you consider separately the parts of an animal body, each will appear to be *intended* for some useful end. There is no evidence that any of them were framed on *purpose* to give pain, or on purpose to be put out of order. Whenever such disorders happen, they may always be referred to some general principle, of apparent utility in other instances.

Obj. 4. It would be better for us, that the accidents, which cause our destruction, should be without pain and without remedy, than that we should be continually exposed to such a variety of evils, as a warning only to preserve ourselves.—But,

Answ. This objection presupposes, what is at least uncertain, that the ills of life exceed the goods. For, if life be desireable upon the whole, it is eligible to suffer those pains,

pains, which are the means of prolonging it.—This may not indeed be applicable to every individual. It is enough, if it hold good with regard to the *usual* state and condition of sensible beings.

The chief observations which have occurred to us on this subject, may be summed up in one general argument; which will be dispatched in a few lines.

Our nature contains *various* capacities of enjoying pleasure, which appear in no respect necessary for any *bad* end. But it contains *no* capacities of suffering pain, which are not apparently necessary for some *good* end. *Useless evil* is a thing never seen, unless in such instances, as are comprehended under a principle *generally* useful. Our nature therefore affords *some* evidence of an intention to produce good: *no* evidence, so far as we have yet seen, of any intention *terminating* in evil.

2. *Of sense and motion.*

I. The bodily *senses* afford a presumptive proof of benevolent intention. They are means of pleasure and of information. Not one

one of them can be taken from us, without evident lofs and harm.

Some of them give *immediate* pleafure, as the fmell and tafte: others may be confidered as *avenues* of pleafure, as the fight and hearing, which lead us to the more refined enjoyment of beauty and harmony*. All of them introduce ideas, the materials of *mental* pleafures: all of them enable us to obtain pleafure, and avoid pain, by informing us of the occafions of each.

Our capacity of perceiving pain cannot be urged in abatement of this evidence. Even the *difagreeable* fenfations, as we have already feen, are not without their ufe. They inform us ufually, what would be prejudicial to us, and ferve to put us on our guard. No man therefore would wifh to be without them.

---

* Primum enim *oculi* in his artibus, quarum judicium eft oculorum, in pictis, fictis, coelatifque formis, in corporum etiam motione, geftu, multa cernunt fubtilius: colorum etiam atque figurarum venuftatem atque ordinem, &, ut ita dicem, decentiam, oculi judicant.—*Auriumque* item eft admirabile quoddam, artificiofumque judicium, quo judicatur——varietas fonorum, intervallo, &c. quæ hominum folum auribus judicantur. Cic. de Nat. Deor. lib. ii. c. 58.

We have no stronger instance of benevolence among men, than the affection of parents to their children. And, would not every parent wish, that his children may have their senses compleat? Would he chuse, that any part of their bodies should be insensible of pain? Certainly not. We see then, that a benevolent affection would lead us, if we ourselves were to determine, to produce animal bodies with the same powers of sensation, which are given by the Author of Nature. We have reason therefore to conclude, that *he* also acts with benevolent intention.

II. The *motive* powers of the body are evidently useful. Without them we should want a considerable part of our active faculties; and be unable to procure the objects, which gratify our senses.

Let it be remembered, however, that the powers of sense and motion are not considered here, as means of *preservation*, but as means of procuring and enjoying a variety of pleasures not *necessary* to us, and of avoiding pains not *destructive* to us. Though the capacity of preserving ourselves should prove nothing; yet the capacity of enjoying these

additional

additional pleasures will evidently prove a benevolent design; for it will prove a design of giving a *happy* existence, distinct from the general intention of providing the *means* of existence. So also every faculty, by which we are enabled to avoid pains *not destructive* to the body, shews, that these pains are contrary to the divine intention; and consequently, that this intention was benevolent.

II.

Of the external causes, which are capable of affecting animal bodies.

These may conveniently be classed under two heads: on one hand the causes of preservation and pleasure; on the other, of destruction and pain.

1. *Of preservation and pleasure.*

On this head we must pursue the same course of reasoning as we did on the last.——It is an undoubted fact, that nature has made a sufficient provision for the sustenance and preservation of animals: so that all of them are capable of obtaining those objects, which

are

are requisite for the support of their lives.—But this fact, of itself, proves nothing. It *could* not be otherwise than it is, whether the intention of our Maker was good or evil.

It is more material to observe, that the causes of preservation are *also* causes of pleasure; and that various means of pleasure are provided, no ways necessary to our preservation.—Thus the several sorts of *food* are made agreeable to the palate; of *flowers* to the smell; of *sound* to the ear; of *visible* objects to the eye: and many also of the works of nature are *beautiful*, as well as useful; and furnished with such qualities, as enable men, in various ways, to multiply their pleasures, and live conveniently and happily.—Now all these means of happiness are presumptions of benevolence. For they apparently tend to produce pleasure; and have no apparent ill tendency in any way whatever.

Obj. It may be said indeed, that these external advantages are too *scarce* for the use of *all*: nay that a very great part of mankind have comparatively but a small share. But,

1st. We may observe, in answer to this objection, that *many* conveniences are *not scarce*.

scarce *. Even the lowest order of men possess more than is necessary for their subsistence, and have also real and constant pleasure in the use of those things which their necessities require: greater perhaps than often falls to the lot of those who are more plentifully provided. Now, this is enough to prove a benevolent intention. The objection only shews, if it shew any thing, that we can *conceive* a constitution of things, in which *greater* benevolence would have appeared: a conclusion with which we have at present no concern.

2dly. Those conveniences which are scarce, are not the most *important* to our happiness. Often indeed they derive all their value from their scarcity †. To make them common, would be to make them contemptible.

3dly. Scarcity is only a relative term, importing that some have more than others.—

---

* Passim jacent *alimenta*, quæ rerum natura omnibus locis deposuit. (Sen. de Conf. ad Helvid. c. 9.)

And again (c. 11.) Nihil homini natura, quod *necessarium* faciebat, fecit *operosum*.

† O miserabilis, quorum palatum, nisi ad *pretiosos* cibos, non excitatur! pretiosos autem non eximius sapor, aut aliqua faucium dulcedo, sed raritas et difficultas parandi fecit. Ib. c. 9.

But

But this circumstance is of no weight in the present question. For there may be just as much benevolence in an unequal, as an equal, distribution of things. It may still be true that God is kind to all, tho' some have received peculiar marks of kindness.

4thly. The word *scarcity* is also relative to human *desires*. There is much want among the rich: much content among the poor. The objection amounts only to this, that men have *some* desires not satisfied; i. e. that they are *not contented.*—But the means are in their own power*.

5thly. That very inequality of which we complain, conduces to the general happiness. The supposition of universal plenty is inconsistent: for it would prevent *labour*, the *necessary* means of plenty.

But this very circumstance may be thought by some to be a fresh cause of complaint. It has been called a *hardship*,

Obj. 2. That the advantages of life are

---

* Cupiditati nihil satis est: naturæ satis est etiam parum. (Sen. de Conf. ad Helvid, c. 11.) Again: Non fortunæ iste vitio, sed suo, pauper est.—Animus est, qui divites facit. See also the story of *Apicius* (c. 10.) cui sestertium centies egestas fuit. I nunc & puta *pecuniæ* modum ad rem pertinere, non *animi*.

not usually to be obtained without *industry*.

In answer to this objection, it might be sufficient to refer the reader to that general law of our nature, which makes the happiness of men depend on their actions. But a more direct answer shall be given under the following observations:

1st. That industry is *no evil*, unless by accident. Both the mind and body are so framed, that a proper exertion of their faculties is not attended with pain; so that there is no *general* inconvenience in annexing this condition to the acquisition of good.

2dly. In those cases, where inconveniences arise from excessive application, *some* compensation is made by the subsequent pleasure of *rest*.

3dly. That constitution of things which makes industry necessary, tends to *prevent* evil, not to produce it. For want of employment would, in many different ways, make men unhappy.

4thly. The exercise of our various faculties, whether for attaining the necessaries or pleasures of life, is naturally *pleasant*. Many indeed of our highest enjoyments confist in action. Therefore this constitution of things, by engaging us to act, promotes our happiness.

5thly. The *improvement* of our faculties depends on the exercise of them; and, without question, the *more* they are improved, the greater good we derive from them.—And,

6thly. It may be just worth mentioning, that good things, of whatever kind, obtained by our own industry, give us peculiar pleasure.

They who are not convinced by these reasons, may attend, if they please, to the most faithful pictures, that are extant, of human life. *Poets* perhaps may describe it more justly than *Philosophers*. To *Virgil* * therefore and *Milton* † let the appeal be made. You may expect in them to find the subject adorned and embellished. But you cannot suppose their descriptions to be *opposite* to truth, and directly repugnant to that *nature*, which they profess to imitate. See then whether the *labours of the country* are painted by those inimitable writers in the same frightful forms,

* Georg. lib. 2. † L'Allegro.

under

under which they appear in the writings of sceptical philosophers. On the contrary, chearfulness and innocence are the most striking features in the admirable portraits they have given us. The husbandman and shepherd are represented as happy even in their daily *toils*; and happy too in the *rest* which succeeds them.—We are told indeed, that industry is but ill suited to the natural *indolence* of man. But it may be said, with greater appearance of truth, that idleness is ill suited to his natural activity. If some men are too indolent; others are too busy. The generality *love* to be employed: and they, whose condition in life places them above the *necessity* of labouring, usually impose on themselves a *voluntary* labour, in one kind or other, under the name of *pleasure*.—One would have thought, that men who have a taste for French books, and French manners, could not have been altogether unacquainted with the sentiment of *ennui*; of which that restless people talk so much, and which, above all things, they profess to dread.

Obj. 3. Industry itself is not *secure* of its reward. The man who labours to support himself

himself and his family, may yet want not only the pleasures and conveniences, but even the *necessaries* of life.

This circumstance however affords no presumption of malevolence. For,

1st. According to the *general* course of nature, industry is the appointed means of obtaining all the advantages of life: and here, as in other instances, we are to judge of a design from its regular and *customary* effects. The exceptions only shew, that it is *imperfectly* executed.

2dly. The wants, which arise from these accidental disappointments, are not unfrequently the occasion of good: as affording room for beneficent actions, which, in many different ways, promote our happiness.

But it is needless to pursue this objection any farther. For this seeming irregularity proceeds from two causes, to be considered in another place: viz. the mutual dependence of mankind, and the uniform government of the material world.

2. *Of destruction and pain.*

1. Experience shews, that a variety of external causes are capable of *destroying* us. In the air, lightning, cold, heat, pestilence; on

the earth, poisons, wild beasts, serpents: under the earth are laid up the materials, which produce eruptions, and earthquakes: the water also may be fatal to land-animals: accidental causes are innumerable. Every part of nature contains, as it were, the seeds of destruction.

It is needless to insist on the possible, or probable, uses, which some, or all, of these things are capable of serving. At all events they afford no presumption of malevolence. For all animals are designed to *die*: the *manner* of dying is immaterial.

2. It is equally evident, that many external causes are capable of producing *pain*. But it is not evident, and not probable, that any one of them was *designed* to produce it; unless with a view to our preservation and happiness. In many instances pain gives us notice of danger; the rest are accidental consequences of good general laws; of laws which cannot be altered without greater harm.

On the whole, we may affirm, that the inanimate parts of the creation furnish us with many advantages, not apparently necessary to any *ill* design: and expose us to no disadvantages, but what are either directly
subservient

subservient to *good*, or accidental consequences of *laws* evidently beneficial. They afford therefore *some* presumption of benevolence, *none* of malevolence.

It may not perhaps be useless, in this place to recollect the circumstances, within and without us, which have afforded us presumptions of divine benevolence. The force of them in this contracted view may more distinctly appear.

RECAPITULATION.

1. The *Appetites* and *Senses*, being immediately necessary to the preservation of the individual, and continuance of the species, are so far no marks of benevolence. But the capacities we enjoy of receiving *agreeable* sensations imply a *farther* design than this. For the ends just mentioned might have been as fully accomplished by painful sensations only; or, it may be, without any sensations at all. Whereas,

1st. The gratification of our *appetites* not only removes pain, but gives positive pleasure.

2dly. The senses of *sight* and *hearing* are avenues both to their proper pleasures, and to others; as of beauty, and harmony.

3dly.

3dly. All the senses enable us to *find* and to *attain* objects of agreeable sensation, and to avoid the contrary.

It is needless to apply this reasoning to our motive powers. They are not only necessary to our preservation, but they contribute greatly to our pleasure.

We conclude therefore, on the whole, that the constitution and frame of our bodies affords a strong presumption of benevolence.

II. In like manner, the corresponding provision of *external* things may also be consider'd as necessary to the preservation of life. We could scarce subsist, especially in the colder climates, if materials were not provided us for clothes and houses: and we are incapable of subsisting at all without food.

But, tho' no conclusion can be drawn from the bare supply of our necessities, yet the *liberal* * supply of them is a consideration of

---

* Sed illa quanta benignitas naturæ, quod tam *multa* ad vescendum, tam *varia & jucunda*, gignit? neque ea uno tempore anni, ut semper & novitate delectemur & copiâ. Cic. de Nat. Deor. lib. ii, c. 53.

Neque enim *necessitatibus* tantummudò nostris provisum est, usque in *delicias* amamur. Sen de Benef. lib. iv. c. 5.—But see the whole of the 4th, 5th, and 6th chapters.

great

great weight. The provision, which is made, of a variety of objects, *not* necessary to life, and ministring only to our pleasures; and the properties given to the necessaries of life themselves, by which they contribute to pleasure *as well* as preservation: these things plainly shew a farther design than that of giving us existence; a design of giving us a *happy* existence.

III.

Of the human mind.

The faculties of the mind may not improperly be reduced to three: the understanding, the will, and the passions.

1. *Of the understanding.*

1. This word, in its widest sense, comprehends all the various modes of thought: viz. the powers of imagining, remembering, comparing, compounding, abstracting.—These are indifferent in their application; being occasions, as it may happen, either of pleasure or pain. Yet since the manner of applying them depends on our own choice;

choice; and it is most likely we should chuse to employ them for our own benefit: they are so far presumptions of benevolence in the Author of Nature.—Thus, for instance,

Imagination is of evident advantage to us. For, besides that it has some pleasures peculiar to itself, it is the necessary *means* both of obtaining pleasure, and avoiding pain; without it, no schemes could ever be formed for the direction of our conduct.

The *memory* of past events helps us to judge of future; and to discern the consequences of different ways of acting, proposed to our deliberation.

The powers of *comparing, compounding,* and *abstracting,* are many ways useful to us; particularly as to them we owe the inestimable advantages of *speech* and *reason*[*]; by which

---

[*] Jam verò *animum* ipsum *mentemque* hominis—ex quo *scientia* intelligitur, quam vim habeat, qualis sit: quâ ne in Deo quidem est res ulla præstantior. Cic de Nat. Deor. l. ii. c. 59. And again, Jam verò domina rerum—*eloquendi* vis, quam est præclara, quamque divina? Ib.

The whole of this chapter, and the two next are much to the purpose. Pope and Bolingbroke have paid little attention to a discourse as beautiful as is just.

we are enabled both to form defigns and to execute them.

Add to all thefe powers the *affociation* of ideas: on which feveral of the preceding operations depend; and which therefore cannot but be beneficial in its *general* influence, tho' in fome particular inftances it may chance to miflead us.

In general, we may conclude each of thefe faculties to be advantageous, becaufe the want of any of them would be efteemed a great lofs, and the perfection of all extremely defireable.

11. Underftanding, in the more confined fenfe of the word, is the name of that faculty by which we are enabled to form true conceptions of the parts and properties, efpecially the *relative* properties, of objects prefented to our view: either on the one hand by *analogical* reafoning, grounded on the teftimony of fenfe, or on the other hand by *demonftrative* proof grounded on intuition.

This faculty, at leaft fome degree of it, is neceffary for the prefervation of life. But this could not be the *whole* intention of it. It
was

was evidently designed to promote the *happiness* of life. For,

1st. It is the source of a *peculiar* pleasure, attending the pursuit and discovery of truth.

2dly. It is the necessary instrument of *action*. Without it we should act in vain, or in ways destructive to our happiness. By it we discern the methods of avoiding evil and obtaining good.

3dly. This faculty contributes greatly to our happiness by making one man agreeable and useful to another.

But the true value of it may best be estimated by the misfortune of *losing* it. Few persons, on this head, would be of the same mind with Him in the poet, who thought it an injury to be restored to his right senses.

2. *Of the Will.*

This faculty also was *intended* for our good; and is therefore an instance of benevolence in the Author of our beings. For,

1st. That constitution of nature, which makes us *active* beings, enables us to follow the

Divine Benevolence asserted, &c. 45

the dictates of the understanding; and by so doing, both to avoid evil, and to obtain good.

2dly. We feel a peculiar satisfaction from success in either kind, when we are conscious of owing it to our own conduct. Whatever advantages we acquire by skill, or industry, or virtue, give us double pleasure on reflection.

3dly. Action itself constitutes a main part of our happiness. There is a singular pleasure in chusing for *ourselves*, and in prosecuting the objects of our choice.

4thly. *Virtuous* actions give still a superior happiness; both from our consciousness of desert, and the approbation we obtain, or think we obtain, from other intelligent beings.

Obj. It may be alleged perhaps, that the *imperfection* of human understanding, and the *uncertainty*, which attends the determinations of the will, leave every man's happiness in a *precarious* state. The *fact* cannot be disputed.—The *account* of it will fall more conveniently under another head. It may be better however to run the hazard of some repetition, than to pass it over intirely in this place.

The

The objection, when fully stated, will stand thus.

That constitution of nature, which makes us intelligent and free beings, is the occasion of evil as well as good; perhaps of *more* evil than good. For men hurt, by the abuse of their faculties, both themselves and others: they have *peculiar* pain too from the sufferings they bring on themselves; and they are exposed to remorse and infamy from acting against the interests of society.—It may suffice, at present, to answer to this objection, that,

1st. *More* of men's actions are beneficial, than hurtful.

2dly. The benefit was *intended* by the Author of Nature, the harm was *not* intended. For the harm, as will appear afterwards, always arises from the abuse of some beneficial principle. The *general* frame and constitution of our nature, with the situation and circumstances in which we are placed, *incline* us to a *right* use of our faculties.

3dly. The power of being happy or miserable, *as we will,* is more likely to be the gift of a good than an evil being. For all

men

men *desire* happiness. Therefore all are likely to *pursue* it.

If any force remain in this objection, it belongs to another head: namely, the *temptations* by which men are led to act wrong. The *power* of acting either constitutes or causes our highest enjoyments: and is not, of itself, any cause at all of misery.—Leaving then this part of the objection to its proper place, we need only observe that the *possible* abuse of our faculties is by no means to be put in competition with the good they actually produce. No man, I suppose, would willingly be deprived of them, to avoid the danger of such abuses.

3. *Of the passions.*

The various modes of pleasure and pain which arise from imagination or reflection, are sometimes distinguished into *internal senses affections*, and *passions*. There is no great use in the distinction; and great difficulty in applying it, so as to refer every sentiment to its proper class. I shall therefore comprehend them all under the general name of *passions**.

* See a slight theory of the passions at the end of this treatise.

Now the powers we possess of receiving pleasure or pain *indifferently*, by means of reflexion, may be considered as presumptions either of benevolence or malevolence, according as the *consequences* resulting from such sensations are beneficial or hurtful. But it should not be forgotten, that we receive some pleasures on reflection, which have *no pains* to balance them.—Such are the pleasures received *directly* from all objects, either of imagination or understanding, which appear *great, beautiful,* or *new.*—Such also are the pleasures received *indirectly* from the various modes of *imitation*, constituting what are called the *liberal arts.* The opposite sensations, if there be any, are too insignificant to deserve notice.

The most obvious division of the *passions* is into those which respect *ourselves* and those which respect *other men:* and these last again may be distinguished into *social* and *malevolent* passions. To these several classes must be subjoined the *moral sense,* the appointed guide of them all.

1. *Of*

1. *Of the selfish Passions.*

1. *Self-esteem,* and its *opposite,* are probable means of *pleasure.* For every man has it in his power to enjoy the one, at least some degree of it, and to avoid the other.

They are also evidently *useful:* by exciting us, on the one hand, to enlarge our capacities of doing good, and to apply them properly; on the other, to forbear all such conduct as might disable us from being useful to ourselves and others. These sentiments, when properly regulated, differ but little from what is called a virtuous *pride,* and a virtuous *shame.*

Suppose a *contrary* constitution. Suppose the ordinary frame of the human mind to be, what we sometimes observe in very uncommon perversions of it. Suppose that every man valued himself in proportion to the insignificance or the hurtfulness of his character, and could not reflect without blushing on his inclination or ability to do good—It is easy to see what must be the consequence.

2. Selfish *desires,* and *aversions* may in general be considered as useful and necessary.

They excite us to useful actions, and restrain us from hurtful ones.

In regard to the *objects* of these passions, it must be remembered, that all our desires aim either at pleasure and the means of producing it*, or the means of removing and preventing pain. Hence,

1st. The desire of *property*.---This inclination gives rise to almost all the *business* transacted in private life: i. e. causes all the happiness, arising from the industry of private men.

2dly. The desires of *dominion*, and *liberty*.— The former encourages men to expose themselves to fatigue and danger for the service of others: the latter is a check on those who have *acquired* dominion, and discourages them from abusing it.

3dly. The desire of *honour*. This passion is many ways useful to mankind.

1 It excites us to *deserve* honour, by acquiring the ability, and improving the dispo-

---

* The *customary* means. These, from association, become objects of desire, even when the pleasing effect is no longer expected. Thus men desire *fame*, and, in some sort they desire *property*, even after death.

sition, which nature has given us, to please and to benefit other men.

2d. It renders men *dear* to each other, if they make a proper use of it; and so increases their propensity to acts of kindness and benevolence. —On the other hand,

3. It restrains them from such conduct, as would render them odious or contemptible: such as might either tend to produce evil, or lessen their capacity of doing good.

Our aversions are aimed against pain and its causes, or against those causes which are destructive of pleasure. Hence,

Death is of course an object of aversion; a constitution plainly tending to our preservation, and probably to our pleasure.

It is needless to pursue the other objects of these passions; which are just as many as the different kinds of sensation, and the different causes of each.

Something however must be said of their general *laws:* the principal of which are these three.

1st. They depend jointly on our opinion of the *probability* of an event, and of its *efficacy* in producing pleasure or pain. Despair kills desire.

fire.—This occasions us to apply our endeavours, where they may be useful; and to forbear fruitless pursuits. At the same time it sets us free from useless uneasiness.

2dly. They are more forcibly excited by *particular* pleasures and pains, than by general views.—These last are of uncertain effect, leaving too much to the determination of reason; and could not so safely have been trusted by nature in some of her most important operations.—The observation is peculiarly applicable to such desires as are founded on bodily appetites. The passions grafted on these appetites, and aiming at particular objects, are much more violent; and ought to be so, than the calm desire of our general interest and happiness.

3dly. They are more forcibly excited by *near* than distant objects.—The former are more likely to be within the reach of our endeavours. The next class of passions are,

3. Selfish *joy* and *sorrow*.—These are indifferent at least; as only serving to enlarge the sphere of our pleasures and pains. Nor do these

these *pains* afford any sort of presumption against the divine benevolence. For they are consequences of the powers of *anticipation* and *memory*, both beneficial: together with the power of feeling uneasiness from past or future events; which is also beneficial, since without it neither anticipation nor memory could influence the will. It is to be considered therefore as an *accidental* ill consequence of a good general constitution.—Indeed these powers cannot be taken away without an intire cessation of human action.

Sorrow too, in many kinds, has its *immediate* use; more perhaps than sufficient to be weighed against it. For, while kept under proper regulations, it is a powerful excitement to *action*; prompting us to a vigorous exertion of our faculties, that we may procure either remedies or compensation.

2. *Of the social and malevolent passions.*

1. *Respect* and *love* are useful by rewarding and encouraging men's ability and inclination to do good.

Respect affords an encouragement to the acquisition of useful talents: restrains men from giving offence, and excites them to please those, who are able to serve or to hurt them.

Love, in *general*, is a pleasing sentiment; and is also a cause of benevolence.—The particular *kinds* of love are evidently beneficial.

1st. *Conjugal* love promotes the ends of marriage: restrains men's desires to a single object, and rewards their fidelity. By these means it promotes such an intercourse between the sexes, as is most beneficial to society.

2dly. *Parental* love rewards the care and fatigue of the parent in providing for his offspring, as well as in preserving and educating them. By these means help is obtained for those, who most want it.—It is obvious too, that the affections of children to parents are not *reciprocal*. This would have been an unnecessary precaution: for the parent usually wants not the assistance of the child.

3dly.

3dly. Love, arising from any kind of personal *merit*, is an encouragement to merit: and love to *benefactors* rewards and encourages beneficence.

4thly. Love of *acquaintance*, besides that we may suppose it to be included under the last head, makes men most *inclined* to do good, where they are most able to do it: and encourages, because it rewards, a frequent intercourse among them.

2. *Contempt* and *hatred* discourage and punish men's inability to do good, or their inclination to do harm.

Contempt gives uneasiness to the objects of it: and this uneasiness excites them very powerfully to remove the cause of it; by correcting, so far as they can, the qualities which produce it, and acquiring some degree of credit and consideration in the world.

Hatred, though a painful, and sometimes a hurtful, sensation, yet in the intention of nature is beneficial.—For,

1st. A general hatred of *bad men* is a constant discouragement to hurtful actions.

2dly. Hatred arising from *personal* injury is a defence to each individual. For both the hatred itself and its consequences strike a terror into those, who *wish* to injure.

3dly. *No* such passion *usually* arises towards *benefactors* or *strangers*, where it would be evidently hurtful: it arises only on the appearance of *harm* done or intended, or good neglected to be done; in which cases it must be generally beneficial.

There is only one exception to this rule, viz.

Hatred, arising from competition, or comparison. But this seems only an accidental consequence of a good general constitution. For hatred *usually* arises, and ought to arise, towards those who give us *pain:* though, in this particular instance, the good effect of it may appear more doubtful than in others.— It is not however altogether without advantage: as serving to increase *emulation*; i. e. a laudable desire of raising ourselves to a level with others, if not of surpassing them in useful talents.

3. *Benevolent*

3. *Benevolent* defires and averfions, with the hopes and fears, joys and forrows, that attend them, are a very material part of this fubject. The *general* utility of thefe fentiments admits of no difpute; they give every man an *intereft* in the happinefs of others, and by confequence excite him to do good, and to forbear evil.

The particular *laws* of this paffion are alfo beneficial.—Thus,

1ft. *Compaffion* is made ftronger than the oppofite fentiment. For the *miferable*, not the happy, need our affiftance.

2dly, Compaffion itfelf is not *invariable*. The *feelings* of it decreafe, as the *habits* produced by it increafe: i. e. the uneafy fenfation is made to abate, in proportion as it becomes lefs neceffary.

3dly. The *oppofite* fentiment is alfo variable; but in a contrary direction. The pleafure we feel from the happinefs of others *increafes* with our habits of beneficence.

4thly. The pain of compaffion is attended with agreeable reflexions. We are told by an excellent judge, that the very *tears* of virtue are

are pleasing: and this pleasure is, in most cases, sufficient to balance the pain; and prevent us from checking a sentiment so useful to society.

5thly. Benevolence is produced and increased by respect and love: it is lessened or destroyed by contempt and hatred. This constitution serves to mark out *particular objects* of our affection: which would otherwise be weak, because it would be general. And that these objects are *properly* marked, no one can doubt, who considers the *causes*, on which the passions abovementioned are found to depend. By them we are prompted to do good to those who best deserve or most want it; and to *attempt* good, where our endeavours are most likely to succeed.

4. *Malevolent* desires and aversions, tho' always painful, and sometimes hurtful, yet, in the intention of nature, are beneficial.— The same causes which produce *hatred*, produce *ill-will*, which is the consequence of hatred: and both these passions, under proper regulations, promote the general good.

When

When we wish ill to others from a principle of *indignation* against vice, or even *resentment* of personal injuries; the sentiment leads us to promote the interests of society by opposing or punishing bad men.

When our ill-will proceeds from competition; it stimulates us the more to acquire those advantages to ourselves, for which we *envy* others: or to avoid the disadvantages, which in them we behold with pleasure. And this was pretty plainly the intention of nature. For, *independently* of such competition, the pleasure of others gives us *no* pain, & v. v.; unless in persons whom we are used to consider as private or public enemies: nor do we feel in *any* case the sentiments of envy and malice, where those sentiments would be altogether *useless*; as, for instance, when we reflect on the talents or success of others, in circumstances totally *unlike* our own.

Obj. But whatever advantage may arise from our malevolent passions, they are supposed to give unnecessary pain, and to occasion unnecessary mischief; for that the selfish and social passions, under the direction of reason,

reason, are sufficient for producing the same ends. Our regard to others, as well as ourselves, will excite us to repel or punish hurtful actions; and our reason will enable us to discern the consequences of such actions, and to guard against them.

In answer to this objection, it is to be observed,

1st. That men *will not* be engaged by these motives, to repell or punish ill actions, when the mischief to be expected from them is either *distant* or *general*.

2dly. That these motives, if they wait for the direction of reason, will operate too *slowly*, and so the opportunities of exertion will often be lost.

3dly. That the resistance and punishment may often be prevented by the *opposition* between social principles and selfish.

4thly. That men are likely to be restrained from prosecuting or punishing offenders by *indolence* and *compassion*.

5thly. That the supposed utility of malevolent passions is fully confirmed by experience.

ence. In the present state of things, *neglect* in resisting or punishing is just as frequent, as *excess*. Remove the influence of indignation and resentment, and it will become much *more* frequent, evidently to the harm of society.

I am sensible, after all, that a writer must lie under great disadvantage, who speaks one word in favour of such odious passions, as *hatred* and *malevolence*. But are not men misled in this instance, as in others, by the imperfection of *language?* A good man, it is supposed, *never hates*, never bears *ill-will* to his neighbour. But the fallacy lies here, that when these sentiments are confined within reasonable bounds, the obnoxious *names* are not given them. Sure it is, that no human breast is free from them; and were they totally banished the world, the mischiefs of such a change would probably be more, and greater, than is usually apprehended.

3. *Of the Moral Sense.*

This *sentiment* (it is seldom, I confess, caled a *passion*) is undoubtedly beneficial. When applied to ourselves, it rewards our virtues, or punishes our vices. When applied to others, it directs our love and hatred, our benevolence and malevolence, to proper objects.

But it is chiefly important, as applied to ourselves: by exciting us to gratify our benevolent inclinations, and rewarding our compliance; and by discouraging us from giving way to other inclinations, when they interfere with these: also by deciding the contest between inconsistent passions, and enabling us to preserve our minds in tranquillity: also by making our conduct *uniform*; that the occasional impulses of passion may not engage us in contrary pursuits, and unavoidable disappointments: lastly, by increasing our attention to distant and general objects, and repressing the violence of particular desires and aversions, which might lead us to neglect our true happiness.

Some persons, misled, I suppose, by the abuse of words, allow no such sentiment to *exist* in the human mind. But no one, we may presume, who admits the *reality*, will dispute the *use* of it.

Not only the sentiment itself, but the *degree* of it, is what it ought to be. We may imagine perhaps that a *higher* degree would be still better; a more effectual guard to our own virtue, and a more powerful restraint on the conduct of other men. But, supposing only our understanding and passions to continue the same in *all other* respects, the change proposed would be a change for the worse. For it would render our esteem of others very difficult, and our self-esteem impossible. Should you think to avoid this inconvenience by increasing only the sense of *moral good*, without increasing the sense of *moral evil* (a thing perhaps impracticable), men would become less cautious of their conduct, and less attentive to their moral improvement. But this is a subject to be resumed in another place*.

* Some writers have imagined, that no conclusions can be drawn from the state of the passions for, or against, Divine Benevolence; because they are not *innate*, but *acquired*. This is frivolous. If we are so framed, and placed in such circumstances, that all these various passions *must* be acquired; it is just the same thing as if they had been planted in us originally. It is true, indeed, they may fall into an *unnatural* state; a state contrary to their *usual* course, and to the intention of our Maker. But that is quite another matter; and will immediately come under a distinct consideration.

Having

Having thus gone through the consideration of the *several* passions, it may be proper to attend to the objections which are made to *all* of them. Of these the most material are the two that follow.

Obj. First, that all our passions, even while they remain in their *natural* state, often give occasion to wrong *conduct*. For that they excite indifferently in *all* circumstances, even in those where they are not to be gratified without damage to ourselves or others.

But to this objection there needs no other answer, than that God governs the world by general laws; a point to be considered at large hereafter.

Obj. 2. It is alledged that all our passions are liable to *abuse*; and that such abuse gives occasion to great mischief, both private and social. The fact indeed is certain; but the objection may be answered in various ways.

1st. The *power* of abusing our passions is a part only of that general dispensation, which makes human happiness depend on human conduct.

2dly. The *actual* abuse proceeds in a great degree from the *imperfection* of our *understanding*

ing; a circumstance, as will afterwards appear, of no weight in the present question.

3dly. These abuses appear to be *accidental* only, not intended by the Author of Nature [*]: Nay, they are plainly *contrary* to his intention: and one part of the harm arising from them serves as a *penalty*; obliging men, in some degree, to *restrain* such abuses in themselves and others. Now, it is from the *customary* and natural state of the passions, not from occasional variations, that we are to collect the design with which they are given us.

4thly. Even these accidental abuses are often *remedied*. For the abuse of one passion frequently corrects the abuse of another: and the excess of a passion in one person frequently balances the defect of it in another.

5thly. The *general* state of the passions is what it ought to be. The *direction* of each is usually right: and the *degree* of each is comparatively right. No one can be considerably weakened, through the whole human species, without great harm, supposing all the

---

[*] Non idcircò (Cic. de Nat. Dor. lib. 3. c. 28.) non optimè nobis à Diis esse *provisum*, quod multi eorum beneficio *perversè* uterentur.

rest to remain as they are. Nor is the force of the passions too great, when taken *all together*. Were the amount of them less, thro' the whole race of mankind, and we were to approach so much the nearer to the apathy of the Stoics: this supposed reformation of our nature would neither make us more useful nor more happy; but, on the contrary, would deprive us of the chief joys of life, and the most powerful springs of human action *.

We have now gone through our enquiry into the various powers of the human mind; and have examined separately, what presumptions they afford of good or ill intention in the Author of Nature: and the result has been, that the understanding, the will, and the passions, are each of them adapted to good *ends*, tho' *accidentally* indeed the occasion of evil. Yet this, it seems, is not sufficient. There are some writers who object to the frame of our nature, not on account of its *unfitness*, but its *imperfection*. I will first state the objection, and then examine the force of it.

* Ἀφαιρεῖσθαι γὰρ ἡμῶν ἄλλη τὴν ἐκ τῷ φιλεῖσθαι καὶ φιλεῖν εὔνοιαν, ἢν παντὸς μᾶλλον διατηρεῖν ἀναγκαῖον. Plut. Conf. ad Ap.

General

General objections.

It is alledged, that our *bodies* are exceedingly *frail*; so that our happiness is in continual danger of interruption from external accidents; some from our own misconduct; some from the misconduct of others; some without any fault, either in us or them. Now why, it is said, are we exposed to so much hazard? Why placed within the reach of innumerable causes of mischief, which we are too blind to avoid, and too weak to withstand? Even with the utmost care and vigilance, it is many times impossible for us to escape them; or to support ourselves under them. Yet God might, if he had pleased, have secured us from them all. He has *not* pleased: therefore he is not benevolent.

The mind too, we are told, as well as the body, is manifestly defective. Its powers are contracted and limited, to a degree which defeats, in a great measure, the main ends for which they are said to have been given us.— Our *reason*, we know, is often unable to direct us to what is good: often exposes us to mistakes,

miſtakes, which lead to evil*.———The *moral faculty* itſelf is liable to be *miſled* by ſuch miſtakes. Even when it is rightly directed, it is *inſufficient*; being too weak to prevail againſt the appetites and paſſions. Now all the conſequences of this imperfect conſtitution were diſtinctly foreſeen by the *Author* of it; and he might, if he had pleaſed, have given us ſo high a degree of underſtanding as would have rendered us infallible; and ſo quick a moral ſenſe as would have rendered us impeccable. Yet, tho' he *ſaw* the miſchiefs which would ariſe from human imperfection, and might have prevented them, he did not *chuſe* to prevent them. The ill therefore which followed was *intended* by him: and it may reaſonably be concluded, that he framed and conſtituted us as we are, with a *deſign* of making us vicious and miſerable.

I believe it will not be denied, that I have given this objection its full force. Yet we

---

* Sentit domus uniuſcujuſque ſentit forum ——ut, quemadmodum ratione recte fiet, ſic ratione peccetur. See this, and much more, alledged by Cotta in Cic. de Nat. Deor. lib. 3. c. 27.

Again (c. 31.) In hominum vitiis ais eſſe culpam. Eam dediſſes hominibus ratione, quæ vitia culpamque excluderet.

shall soon see, that it has no force at all, but what arises from presumption and folly.

For in the first place, the objectors will never be able to prove, what they assert with the utmost confidence, that God *might* have made us more perfect than we are. Most sure it is, that he can do all things possible. But are *we*, in any degree, competent *judges* of the bounds of possibility? We can hardly stir one step farther than we have *experience* for our guide. When this guide fails us, we have no bottom to stand upon; unless we will trust to a principle very apt to mislead us, that whatever man can imagine, God can effect. But,

2dly, If we allow them the possibility of greater perfection, they will still be unable to prove the *expedience* of it. For who can take upon him to say, that the production of a *less perfect* being may not be best for the *universe?* We see, in this system, the advantage, and even necessity, of *subordination*. May it not be equally necessary to the good of the whole? We need not indeed to stop here. For,

3dly, It *may* be best for man in particular, that his *first* state should be an imperfect one. This appears probable even from analogy.

Men would be unfit for the part allotted to them in their *riper* years, if they were not trained up in the discipline of *childhood*. May not, in like manner, the *whole* of our present life be a state of discipline? a necessary preparation for a higher state? If so, our complaints will amount to nothing more, than that we are children first, before we are men.—Nay, those very imperfections, of which we complain, are, in one view, of *evident* importance to us: I mean, as they afford room for the acquisition of virtuous habits; habits of *resolution* and *attention*. Attention could have no place at all, if our judgement were infallible; for perfect security excludes all care: and *resolution* would be useless, if we had no difficulties to surmount. And may not the virtues, which are thus acquired, be the necessary foundation of our supreme happiness? May not our passing with prudence and fortitude thro' the uncertainties and dangers of this present state, be the necessary means of attaining that *higher* degree of perfection, to which we ignorantly and presumptuously put in our claim, before we are qualified to receive it? It is plainly *not* the method of nature,

ture, in other parts of the creation, to obtain her ends *inſtantaneouſly*. Perhaps therefore perfection *cannot* be thus attained; but men muſt be gradually formed to that capacity and temper, which are to make them happy for ever.

Even if all theſe conjectures ſhould fail (which are ſurely more probable than any thing that can be ſet againſt them), ſtill the argument alledged will be found inconcluſive, For,

4thly. The evils to which we are expoſed in this imperfect ſtate appear to be *accidental*, not natural, effects of our frame and condition. Every part of the body, and every faculty of the mind, was evidently *deſigned* for the good it produces: but there is no appearance that any of them was deſigned to produce evil; both becauſe the production of evil affords a leſs *certain* proof of intention, and becauſe alſo it is leſs *frequently* produced by any aſſignable principle in human nature*.—Let us ſuppoſe

---

* Thus, for inſtance, the *ſtomach* was deſigned for digeſtion, not indigeſtion; the *eyes* for ſeeing, not for ſmarting; the *feet* for walking, not for the pains of the gout.

suppose however, for a moment, that the ills of life were actually *included* in the divine intention; yet this hinders not, but that our nature may have been constituted by a wise and good being. For,

5thly, Should we admit, that the bodies of men *might* have possessed a greater degree of strength and firmness, without loss or harm in any other respect; yet our present frailty will prove only a *limitation* of benevolence, not a total *want* of it, in the Author of Nature. Should we admit further, that our intellectual and moral powers *might* have been advanced to a higher degree of perfection, without defeating any good purpose whatever; yet the defects of which we complain, will only shew a *deficiency*, as we might fancy, in the divine goodness: they will afford no presumption of *malevolent* intention. It avails nothing to say, that this imperfect constitution gives occasion to *evil*. For it was *kindness*, not malice, to intend a *mixed* system with a supe-

---

So again the passion of *shame* was designed to prevent disgraceful actions, not surely to influence an unhappy mother to the murder of her own child.

rior tendency to good: juſt as much as to produce a *ſmaller* degree of good, unmixed with evil; which, I preſume, no one would have denied to be a clear proof of benevolence. If you require all the ill to be removed, and yet *all* the good to continue; you require in effect *more* good, i. e. a higher degree of benevolence. But the arguments, by which we prove the Divine Benevolence to a certain degree, are not overturned by objecting, that a *greater* degree is conceivable. I am now arguing on the very unreaſonable ſuppoſition, that human conception is the meaſure of divine power. Yet the objector, when poſſeſſed of every advantage which this ſtrange ſuppoſition can give, has no way of ſupporting himſelf, but by an argument as void of ſenſe as it is of gratitude; "God has given us *nothing*, becauſe he has *more* to give:" an argument, which proves equally againſt *every* imaginable condition of being; and therefore proves, in reality, againſt *none*.

"Not ſo, it will be ſaid, for God may, if he pleaſes, give *all*: may totally *exhauſt* his own power by forming the *beſt ſyſtem poſſible*. Had

Had he done this, there would have been nothing left either to afk or to wifh."—But neither will this fuppofition have any better fuccefs in eluding the force of our prefent argument.

For why may we not fay, with the philofophers of a neighbouring nation*, the beft fyftem poffible has *actually* taken place? Let him, that *can*, comfute the affertion. While it remains *unconfuted*, it will be found an invincible obftacle to all arguments againft the goodnefs of God.

We might here conclude this branch of our inquiry; but the fubject of human nature is fo very important, that it may not be improper to collect fome of the preceding obfervations into a fingle point of view. For this purpofe the following fhort abftract is laid before the reader. It is chiefly taken from a book lefs known, and lefs valued, than

---

* See the *Theodicée* of M. *Leibnitz*: with whom alfo agrees Balbus in Cic. de Nat. Deor. l. 11. c. 34.

Cujus quidem adminiftratio nihil habet in fe quod reprehendi poffit: ex iis enim naturis quæ erant, quod effici *optimum* potuit, effectum eft.

it deserves, Mr. Hutcheson's Treatise on the Passions.

Remarks on the utility of our senses and passions.

1. The appetites of hunger, thirst, sleepiness, prevent us from neglecting the means of preservatn; inform us of the times, when these means are to be used; and overcome our aversion to labour in the attainment of them.

2. The appetites of the sexes prevent us from neglecting the means of continuing the species; and overcome the apprehension of expence and trouble in the care and education of children.

3. The sense of external pain is, in a good measure, necessary to restrain us from hurting ourselves: the pains of sickness, to put us on seeking for proper remedies. Nor is the degree of these pains too acute. For we see, in fact, they are not always *sufficiently* acute, to answer their ends compleatly.

4. The *various tribes* of selfish affections and passions are all the result of these few necessary

cessary principles: and therefore this part of the constitution of our nature affords us no arguments against the benevolence of its Author.

5. Were the *selfish* appetites and passions left alone, we should be greatly indisposed to acts of beneficence, and frequently engaged in acts of a contrary tendency. They are properly balanced therefore by a *sympathy* with others: whence it comes to pass, in a variety of cases, that *their* interests become *ours*; and excite similar passions in our minds. This sympathy is strongest where it is most needful: i. e. in the *misfortunes* of others. The pain we feel from *compassion* is of evident advantage to mankind.

6. The opposite passion of *resentment* is necessary to restrain injustice, (the effect of selfish passions frequently, and sometimes of *social*) by making it dangerous to the aggressor.

7. *Shame* and *remorse* either restrain us from ill conduct, or lead us to repent and reform. They cannot be thought too strong. For they are often found ineffectual.

8. Any

8. Any increase of the *selfish* passions, without a higher degree of understanding, would make men unfit for society: and, on the other hand, an increase of the *social* passions would qualify us to be heroes of romance, rather than reasonable beings.

IV. *Of the mutual dependence between man and other animals.*

Men unquestionably receive benefit, in various ways, from the brute creation: and they, in return, from the skill and industry of men*. Now

1. This is an argument of God's benevolence to *men*: which appears by his making so plentiful a provision for their convenience and happiness.

---

* Accedit etiam ad nonnullorum animantium ——conserva-tionem et salutem hominum etiam sollertia et diligentia. Nam multæ——pecudes sunt, quæ sine procuratione hominum salvæ esse non possunt. Cic. de Nat. Deor. lib. 11. c. 52.

In C. 65. of the same book, Balbus proves, on the other hand, Ipsas bestias hominum gratiâ generatas esse. He instances in sheep, dogs, oxen, swine, &c.

2. It

2. It is also a proof of his benevolence to *inferior* creatures. For inanimate and vegetable substances might have answered *our* uses just as well. The addition therefore of life and sense shews, it was God's intention to give room for *more* happiness in his creation; and, the care we take of brute animals being the *condition* of our deriving advantage from them, it appears to have been farther intended that such care should be taken.

Obj. Some brutes are useless; others destructive to man; and they, on the other hand, suffer and die for *his* convenience. To this may be answered,

1st. That the *uselessness* of any part of the animal creation, only shews the dependence not to be *universal*. Still these very animals, however useless to *us*, afford arguments of divine benevolence: for they are all of them made capable, in some degree, of enjoying pleasure.

2dly. The brutes, which are *destructive* to men, afford no argument of malevolence.—For it was not the intention of nature that

men

men should be *immortal*; and the *manner* of their dying is a circumstance of little moment.

3dly. To the remaining part of the objection we say; Those brutes, which are useful to man, derive in general *more* good than ill from their connexion with him. If the lives of some of them are shortened by it, they have, while they live, care taken of them, and a better provision is made for them in all respects, than they were capable of making for themselves. Add to this, that a much greater *number* of these animals is supported by human industry, than could possibly have subsisted, if the earth had remained without cultivation.

It is true, indeed, that men sometimes *abuse* the power they have over animals. But what power will they not abuse?

V. *Of the mutual dependence of mankind.*

This constitution affords a strong presumption of divine benevolence.

1. Because it gives room for the exercise of human *virtue*.

2. Because

2. Becaufe it gives rife to the pleafures of *friendfhip*, and to thofe which we derive from the *efteem* and *benevolence* of other men.

3. Becaufe it unites men in *fociety*; and fo leads them on to every enjoyment they receive from their mutual intercourfe.

Still indeed we lie open to the objection fo often repeated, and fo applicable to almoft every circumftance of our condition in this world, viz.

Obj. Men are continually *abufing* their power over others; and thus numbers fuffer by one man's fault.

The objection however may be anfwered in many different ways.

1ft. The *faults* of men were not *intended* by their Creator. All inftances of mifconduct in them are contrary to *his* will; and *almoft* all are contrary to their own intereft, which naturally all men purfue.

2dly. All our faults arife either from the conftitution of the human *mind*, or the *external* circumftances of our fituation; both which have been already vindicated.

3dly. The good effects of focial intercourfe far overbalance the ill; and therefore thefe can only weaken, not deftroy, the force of the argument.

Hitherto we have fought for arguments in the different *parts* of the conftitution of nature, and the *particular laws* to which each of them is fubject. The next object of enquiry will be thofe *more general* laws, which extend thro' God's *whole* adminiftration: and thefe alfo will be found to fuggeft probable arguments of a benevolent intention in the Author of Nature; certainly to afford *no* prefumption of a *contrary* intention.

END OF THE FIRST PART.

PART II.

THIS part of our inquiry, agreeably to the plan propofed, will comprehend an anfwer to the following queftions.

1. Whether the more general laws of divine adminiftration afford any prefumption of good, or ill, intention in the Deity.

2. Whether any additional evidence arifes, on either part, from the uniformity and conftancy with which God's laws are adminiftered.

3. Whether the continual oppofition made to divine adminiftration by human agents, afford us any caufe to doubt of the benevolence of our Maker.

I. *Of the more general laws of divine adminiftration.*

The principal of thefe laws are three; all of which, at firft fight, may create fome fufpicion

picion at least of a want of benevolence in the Author of Nature.

1. That the happiness of men is made to depend on their *actions*.

2. That they are excited to perform these actions by *punishments*, as well as rewards.

3. That, in *both* ways, they are often excited to *hurtful*, as well as beneficial, actions.

1. That the happiness of men is made to depend on their actions.

This law, whatever other conclusions may be drawn from it, will certainly afford no proof of *malevolence*. It is true, indeed, that men's happiness or misery is, to a great degree, put in their own power. But power, of itself, has no more tendency to ill than good; and therefore no inference, of either kind, can with certainty be gathered from this part of the constitution of nature. The presumption however seems rather to lie on the side of benevolence. To give the *ability* of obtaining good, is, in effect, to give the *good itself*. Our *imagination* at least, if not our *understanding*, readily assents to this conclusion: and, if we look no farther than sensible objects, *experience*

perience alſo will juſtify us in aſſerting, that in the ordinary courſe of things, he who *can* be happy, *will* be ſo.

But, if this rule of God's government be no proof of his malevolence, it may ſeem at leaſt to prove, that he is *not* benevolent. For had happineſs been the end propoſed by our Creator, we are ready to think, he would have provided ſome *certain means* to make us happy. Human actions are *uncertain*. Therefore happineſs was *not* the end propoſed.

This is plauſible; yet, when examined to the bottom, will be found to have no real weight. For

1ſt. The argument proves *too much*. It leads to a total rejection of all final cauſes. Even the ſucceſſive exiſtence of plants and animals muſt no longer be imputed to deſign. For we ſee, in many particular inſtances, that the means provided fail of ſucceſs.

2dly. The uncertainty complained of could no way have been prevented, without making it *impoſſible* for us to attain to any conſiderable degree of happineſs. Were the advantages we enjoy in the preſent ſtate of things independent on our actions, no man would act: and,

and, if you destroy all the *active* pleasures of our nature, you destroy by far the most valuable part of our enjoyments; all, indeed, that makes the condition of a man better than that of a brute. I might have said, *more* than all. For even brutes, as it seems, have some pleasure from acting.—More particularly,

That a man's happiness should depend on his *own* actions, was plainly necessary, in order to provoke the exertion of his mental faculties; to make him *reason, judge, chuse*: which very acts constitute much of his happiness; improve the pleasures arising from other sources; and fill up those vacancies of sensual gratification, which would otherwise be attended with disgust and uneasiness.

That the happiness of *one* man should depend on the actions of *another*, was necessary, in order to give us the pleasures of *benevolent* actions and passions; of *self-approbation*; of *fame*: all of them principal ingredients in human happiness.

I know not what more can be urged, on the opposite side, unless it should be supposed, that

that another, and a different, fyftem, might have been formed; in which fenfible beings fhould have been no more than *paffive* inftruments; capable of *receiving* pleafures, not of *procuring* them; pleafures to us unknown, and inconceivable *.

But this fuppofition is only a dream. The poffibility of fuch a fyftem, as is here defcribed, cannot be fupported, even by the flighteft proof. We can only reafon from what we *know*; not furely from what we *fancy*. We *know*, that action is a continual fource of happinefs: but we do *not* know, that happinefs

might

---

* Such was the Epicurean paradife. Quod beatum eternumque fit, nec habere ipfum *negoti* quicquam, nec exhibere alteri. — In anfwer therefore to the inquiry, quæ vita Deorum fit? Velleius fays (Cic. de Nat. Deorum, lib. 1. c. 19.) Ea videlicet quâ nihil beatius, nihil omnibus bonis affluentius cogitari poteft. *Nihil enim agit*; nullis occupationibus eft implicatus; nulla *opera* molitur.——In like manner *human* happinefs is placed in animi fecuritate, et in *omnium vacatione munerum*, c. 20.

On all which Cotta remarks, c. 37. Profectò Epicurus, quafi pueri delicati, nihil *ceffatione* melius exiftimat. At ipfi tamen pueri, etiam cum ceffent, exercitatione aliquâ ludicrâ delectantur.

So again Plutarch, ὁ μὲν ἐν εἰπὼν, ὅτι δεῖ τὸν εὐθυμεῖν μέλλοντα μήτε πολλὰ πρήσσειν μήτε ἰδίῃ μήτε ξυνῇ, πρῶτον μὲν ἡμῖν πολυτελῆ τὴν εὐθυμίαν καθίστησι, γινομένην ὤνιον ἀπραξίας.—ἔπειτα κὶ ψευδὴς ἐστι τὸ εὐθυμεῖν τὰς μὴ πολλὰ πράσσοντας. Περὶ εὐθυμίας.

See

might have been attained *without* it. Imagination only, not reason, suggested the idea.

2. That men are excited to act by *punishments*, as well as rewards.

This again is no proof of *malevolence*. For there is room to suppose, and some reason to beleve, that *rewards alone* would be ineffectual. In *human* governments we know and feel that they are. Now *that* evil can be no argument of a *bad* intention, which appears to be necessary for accomplishing a *good* one.— But the necessity of penal sanctions will best appear, if we attend to a particular instance.

It is certain, then, that *rewards only* would have been an insufficient provision for the preservation of the individual, and the continuance of the species. With respect to the *former*, we should have wanted the admonitions of hunger, thirst, and weariness, to inform us of the *times*, when nature demands supply. In *both* cases, if the appetites were removed,

---

See the same writer in his piece Non posse suav. viv. sec. Epicurum. Λυπεῖται δὲ τὸ πρακτικὸν ὅσας ἡδονὰς ἔχει διαλιπῖν. Αὐτοὶ δὲ δὴ σὺ λέγουσιν, ὡς τὸ εὖ ΠΟΙΕΙΝ ἥδιόν ἐστι τοῦ ΠΑΣΧΕΙΝ, and what follows. And again, ταῖς μέθαι τᾶς ψυχῆς χαραῖς—μέγιστος ὑπολείπεται οὖν πράξιων, &c.

men might forbear to use the *means* of preservation, &c. notwithstanding the pleasure annexed. For the pursuit of pleasure in one kind is often prevented by the desire of *different* pleasures. In *both* cases too the appetites seem necessary to engage us in the *labour* and *hazards*, which either procure, or follow, the gratification. To make this still more plain, let us suppose the pleasure of food to be what it is, and all other circumstances to continue; but let the uneasy sensations of hunger be entirely removed: could these sensations be spared without inconvenience? Certainly not. For, 1st, as has been said, they inform us of the *times*, when nature wants a supply. 2dly, they prevent us from *overlooking*, or *forgetting* our sustenance, which we might easily do, when engaged in other pursuits. 3dly, they are requisite to overcome our *indolence*; which otherwise would often prevent the labour necessary for acquiring sustenance.

Should it be proposed to obtain the same ends by increasing the pleasures of gratification, you will increase also the temptation to excess. If you would have the pleasure stop at the very *point*, where gratification becomes hurtful;

hurtful; you require such a constitution of body, as you have no reason to suppose within the bounds of possibility. Or, admitting it to be possible, who can say that it might not be productive of greater loss or harm? The present constitution *may* be necessary (and *here*, it must be observed; we contend for nothing more) to our perfection and happiness.----Now such creatures as *we* are *could* not be preserved without the appetite of *hunger*: and as for *other* kind of creatures, we are surely not judges of the different ways in which it was *possible* for the Deity to form and preserve animal bodies.

The same method of reasoning, or nearly the same, may easily be applied to all other uneasy sensations, by which we are led to fulfil the ends of nature.—But the reader need not be told, that it is not pretended to give a *full* solution of this difficulty. *Why* God chuses to govern by *penal* sanctions, we know but imperfectly: yet we know enough to discern that these sanctions will furnish no proof against divine benevolence. We see plainly, that, as the *present* system is formed, they are necessary to the most beneficial and important purposes;

purposes: and therefore they afford no degree of evidence against a kind and benevolent intention (already supported by so many clear and strong presumptions) in the Author of Nature.

3. That men are excited to *hurtful*, as well as useful, actions.

This circumstance again may appear, on a slight view, unfavourable to the doctrine of divine benevolence. For it is this part of our constitution, which evidently gives occasion to all the *vice*, and most of the misery, that is in the world.—Yet neither here is the conlusion justly founded *.

For the *general* principles, by which men are excited to action *are* what they *ought* to be. Let them but continue general; and you cannot so much as *imagine* a change for the better. The difficulty then will fall under ano-

---

* Plutarch (against the Stoics) seems to have misapprehended this matter. He insists that vice is *not beneficial*. We allow it. But we maintain that it *springs* from beneficial *principles* ; principles *tending* to good, tho', in some particular instances, giving occasion to evil.

ther

ther head, viz. the *conſtancy* of the laws by which the world is governed.—Or, if any doubt ſhould ſtill remain, the ſubject will be reſumed, when we come to ſpeak of the *oppoſition* made by human beings to the counſels of their Maker.

II.

Of the uniformity of the divine adminiſtration.

It is an undiſputed fact, that the world is governed, to a very great degree, by *invariable* laws: and this rigour of divine adminiſtration has been thought an argument againſt divine benevolence.—The courſe of nature, it is ſaid, never changes. Had this courſe been intended for our benefit, the laws of it would have been *ſuſpended* in every inſtance, where they obſtruct, or defeat, the end propoſed. In fact they are *not* ſuſpended. Our benefit therefore was *not intended*. At leaſt, the harm ariſing from the preſent conſtitution of things, in *ſome* inſtances, is as much a proof of *malevolence*, as the good produced in *other* inſtances of benevolence.

Before

Before an anfwer be given to this allegation, I muft afk, Whether the fufpenfion required, of the laws of nature, be an *apparent*, or an *invifible* fufpenfion. Surely not an apparent fufpenfion, the *prefent* method purfued by Povidence being evidently more advantageous to mankind. Without the *appearance* of uniformity there could be no room for human *fkill*, and no motive to human *action*. Not the former: becaufe fkill of every kind is founded on conftant experience. Not the latter: becaufe no man would ever be induced to act, if he were equally fure, *without* acting, of fuccefs in every undertaking; and he could not *but* be fure, if he faw, that the courfe of nature was continually accommodated to *his* wants and defires.

But, as this is a fubject of fome importance, it may be proper to confider it a little more particularly.—I fay, then, that the happinefs of man depends on the exercife of his faculties: that is, on the right application of his active powers, under the direction of his underftanding. But the underftanding can give *no* direction for our conduct, unlefs we can judge of the effects and confequences of actions

actions proposed to our deliberation: and we only judge of these (we have no other *possible* method of judging) from the effects of *like* actions in times past. If then similar effects do not constantly flow from similar causes, we shall have *no* rule of conduct at all.—Experience of the past is our only guide for the future. We have no other way of knowing that food will nourish, or that arsenic will poison us. We have no other way of discerning any connection between the seed we put into the ground, and the harvest we expect to reap. It is thus we learn, that labour must prepare the soil; that sun and rain will cherish the rising plant, and bring it at length to maturity and perfection. Were not like causes to produce like effects, we could form no judgment at all of future events; and therefore our understanding could never regulate our conduct.

Some perhaps may imagine that all the advantages proposed *might* be obtained without *perfect* uniformity. The objectors, it seems, only demand, that the course of nature should be suspended *occasionally*, when men would lose, or suffer, from its continuance;

ance; and in all other cafes fhould remain invariable. Now here, it may be thought, would be a *general* experience, affording fufficient probability to direct our conduct. Yet, while we enjoyed all the benefit of the prefent conftitution of things, we fhould fuffer none of the harm.

It would not perhaps be eafy for men to agree on the particular cafes in which the laws of nature ought to be fufpended; or for Providence to accommodate them all at once fuitably to their various wants and wifhes.—But, not to infift on this, I anfwer, that, on the fuppofition here made, we fhould learn from experience, that the good fuccefs of all our *defigns* was infallible. For either they would fucceed in the *ordinary* courfe of things, or the courfe of things would be *altered*, to prevent our difappointment. We fhould therefore foon find, that *fkill* and *prudence* were perfectly infignificant, and confequently the very exiftence of defign and contrivance would become in the end *impoffible*. In like manner, we fhould learn from experience, that the objects of our averfion were *conftantly* removed, and our defires *conftantly* gratified, either with, or without, the concurrence of our own *endeavours*; in the one cafe, by the ordinary courfe of things, in the other, by a feafonable deviation from it. We fhould therefore foon difcover, that human action and induftry were altogether *infignificant*; and confequently fhould have no motive for acting at all.

Even a *fecret* fufpenfion of natural laws would be attended with the fame inconvenience, if men once found themfelves *fecure* (no matter by what means) from want, difappointment, and pain of every kind. For they would juft as much, and as confidently, depend on this unfeen interpofition, as in the former cafe on a vifible and extraordinary Providence; and, in either of thefe cafes, they would want the chief enjoyments of human life; all that arife from the exertion of their beft faculties in promoting and fecuring their mutual happinefs.

Shall we ftill be told, that God might *occafionally* deviate in an *unfeen* manner from the general laws of his adminiftration? that he might do this, to a confiderable degree; yet not fo, as to encourage men in *trufting* to thefe extraordinary intetpofitions? and that therefore

fore human skill and industry might still continue, and only be employed with greater success?

I answer—

1st. That, in *proportion* as men owed their success to such secret causes, their skill and their industry would become *less* important. Therefore they would be *less encouraged* to study and pursue the improvement of their happiness: and, in some degree, therefore the same inconveniences would still remain. But

2dly. So far as these secret interpositions are truly proper for us, I see no reason to deny, that God *actually interposes*. For, since, by the very supposition, the deviations, to be made from the ordinary course of nature, are always to remain *undiscovered*; it can never be concluded, that God does *not* deviate, only because no discovery is made.—It is in this sense, that *reason* allows us to hope, and *revelation* authorises us to expect, a *particular providence*. It is in this sense, that we may reasonably promise ourselves success in our *petitions* to Heaven, without looking for miracles: and without that arbitrary assumption, which has been advanced by some very elegant writers

writers*, viz. that the original laws of the univerſe were artificially accommodated to all the future occaſions and wants of every devout petitioner. It is in this ſenſe alſo, that we are promiſed the aſſiſtance of God's *Holy Spirit*: the *effects* of which may appear in a life of piety and virtue; but the *operations* are ſecret, not to be diſtinguiſhed from the workings of our own minds.

To return from this digreſſion, I ſuppoſe it has ſufficiently appeared, that the uniformity, with which God governs the world, is abſolutely *neceſſary* in a diſpenſation of things, adapted to the uſes of an intelligent and active being

III. *Of the oppoſition made by human agents to the ends of divine government.*

It has often been alledged, that the natural ſyſtem, however well and wiſely framed, is liable to be perverted by the folly and wickedneſs of *man*; ſo that the cauſes, which *might* have produced good, are made *in fact*

---

* See Woolaſton, Sect. 5.

the means and instruments of evil*. Now the *intention* of God, we are told, is not to be collected from the *possible* effects of natural causes, but from the effects they are *likely* to produce under human direction: and since men have both a *power* of doing harm, and innumerable *temptations* to do it, those effects must frequently be *evil*. Evil then, as well as good, was *intended* by our Maker.

Here again, as in the last instance, the *fact* is not to be contested. Unfortunately for the race of mankind, it is confirmed to us by daily and hourly experience.——But many things remain to be well considered, before the conclusion drawn from this fact can either be justified or excused.

1st, Let it be observed, that the natural system may be *improved*, as well as perverted, by the conduct of mankind. If its good effects are liable to be obstructed by the weakness and wickedness of human agents, they are capable also of being continued and increased by human skill and virtue: and this advantage should undoubtedly be put in the

---

* Τό γε πολλαχῇ εἶναι ἐργώδη κὶ ἄσκολον τὸν βίον, ἄγαν ἀληθες. Καὶ γὰρ εἰ φύσει τοιοῦτον ἔχει τὸν τρόπον, ὑπό γε ΗΜΩΝ ἐις τοτο πλείας διαφοράς. Plut. Conf. ad Apoll.

balance

balance against such occasional perversions. Probably it may be found sufficient to outweigh the mischief complained of. For men are more likely to use their endeavours for improving and bettering their condition, than to draw unnecessary evils from a system naturally beneficial. The most that can be alledged is, that the present system has a *mixed* tendency; and, if the good preponderate (the *contrary* of which does not appear), such a tendency is surely no proof of malevolence. But this is not all. For

2dly, Both our *power* of doing ill, and our *temptations* to do it, are the result of a wise and good constitution of nature.

1. The *power* is derived from certain general laws of evident good tendency; namely, that each man's happiness is made to depend on his actions; and that, in very many instances, the happiness of one man is made to depend on the actions of another. These laws have been already vindicated; and appear to be inseparably connected with the business and the pleasures of human life. A world, in which nothing depended on ourselves, however it might have suited some imaginary race of beings, would never have suited *mankind*;

kind; or, rather, would have transformed them into other creatures; from intelligent and active beings to beings immersed in sense, and incapable of all higher gratifications.

2. Nor has the other part of the objection been altogether neglected. We all know, by fatal experience, that we have not only the power of doing ill, but are also *tempted* to do it. Yet we have seen, that no inference can be drawn from this confession to the prejudice of divine benevolence; for that the *general* principles of the human mind, notwithstanding accidental variations, are what they ought to be. In single persons, it must be owned, the balance of the passions is very frequently destroyed; seldom indeed preserved with exactness and truth. But then the defects, to be found in one man, are supplied by the excesses in another. So that, if you consider the *whole* species, you will neither find too much, nor too little, of any one principle in the human mind. Indolence and ambition, avarice and sensuality, resentment and compassion, if not in the same persons, yet in different persons, counteract and balance each other. Nor is there a single sentiment

timent implanted in our nature, which can either be increased, or lessened, in the *whole* race of mankind, without loss or harm to the human species; unless indeed you assume a liberty of altering *many* things at a time; of forming a new and fantastic system, perhaps made up of inconsistent parts, and beyond the bounds of possibility itself. So true is that celebrated passage of Cicero, de Nat. Deorum, lib. 2. c. 34. *Siquis corrigere aliquid volet, aut deterius faciet, aut id, quod fieri non potuit, desiderabit.*

These considerations will receive additional force, if there be any ground for what was intimated in the former part of this treatise, that the views of Providence extend beyond the limits of this present life. Many things here carry the *appearance* at least of a state of *trial* and *discipline*; a state not to be conceived without opportunities of doing ill, and temptations to do it. Allow only the present life to be connected with a better, and every objection to divine benevolence ceases of course. Is it not then more reasonable to admit and maintain this connection, than to oppose our visionary difficulties (founded, for the

the most part, on the narrowness of our views, and the obscurity of our conceptions) to those innumerable marks of wisdom and goodness, which shine forth through the whole creation?

But whether we believe, or disbelieve, a life *to come* (a subject on which *revelation* only is capable of giving us *full* satisfaction), one thing is certain, viz. that the *present* life furnishes no reasonable pretence, nor any colourable excuse, for disputing the goodness of our Maker. The *words* of *Cicero*, on this subject, are surely more reasonable than his *practice* : Mala—et impia consuetudo est *contra Deos* disputandi, sive ex animo id fit, sive simulatè. De Nat. Deorum, lib. 2. c. 27.

END OF THE SECOND PART.

PART III.

IT has already appeared, that the present constitution of things affords *many* strong presumptions of a benevolent intention in the Author of Nature; and that *nothing* is to be found, which will justify a *contrary* conclusion, even in the most doubtful and difficult parts of divine administration. It must be owned, however, that the evidence produced would be either subverted or shaken, if full proof could be brought, that, in the *result* of things, these *seemingly* kind intentions have been all frustrated; and that a large overbalance of evil has actually taken place. In *human* works, it is true, the *design* cannot always be inferred from the *effect*. For *men* may be deceived and disappointed. But in *divine*

divine works such mistakes are impossible *. *Particular* evils may arise in a system whose general tendency is good; as we have seen in various instances. But a *prepollency* of evil can be *no* accident. If the *whole world* appear to be little more than a scene of wretchedness and misery, we shall naturally suspect, that nothing better was *intended*. On this supposition, we might be led to doubt, with great appearance of reason, whether it were consistent with the wisdom of God, not to *foresee* the evil; or with his goodness, not to *prevent* it. What Cotta says of *reason* [Cic. de Nat. Deorum, lib. 3. c. 27.] might then be applied to *life itself*, and all the flattering hopes that surround it: Satius fuerit omnino non datam, quam tantâ cum pernicie datam.

But the fact here supposed has never *yet* been proved.—We believe and trust, that it never *will*. Instead of coming to this gloomy

---

* Ubi igitur locus fuit errori Deorum? Nam patrimonia spe bene tradendi relinquimus; quâ possumus falli. Deus falli potuit?—Cotta in Cic. de Nat. Deorum, lib. 3. c. 31.

Plutarch (de rep. Stoic.) justly represents Chrysipppus as inconsistent with himself, when he affirms that the gods ὡς ἐν βέλτιϛα προνοεῖν, yet that men, ὡς ἐν χείριϛα πράττειν.

and

and uncomfortable conclusion [*], we may more reasonably infer from the apparent *intentions* of nature; that the *success* has been answerable: and that good, *prepollent* good, is the result of all.—Were it possibe for us to support this inference by clear and full *experience*, we might form a *decisive* argument for the divine benevolence.—The happiness, we would say, which has in fact been produced by the present system, is much greater than the misery. This happiness has arisen from the *nature* of the system itself; not from foreign, or accidental, causes. It was therefore *intended* by the Author of the system; or the system was formed with a *design* of producing happiness. It appears then that the happiness of created beings is an object *pleasing* in the eyes of their Creator: or, in other words, that he is a *benevolent* Being.

All that needs to be inforced, in this argument, is the fact supposed as its foundation:

---

[*] ἆρά γε δίκης ἑτέρας οἴεσθε δεῖσθαι τὰς ἀναιροῦντας τὴν πρόνοιαν, ἢ οὐχ ἱκανὴν ἔχειν, ἐκπίπτοντας ἑαυτῶν ἡδονὴν ἢ χαρὰν τοσαύτην; Plut. Non posse suav. vivi sec. Epicurum.

And again, τῆς μὲν εὐτυχίας τὸ ἥδιστον κωλύεσιν, ταῖς δὲ δυσυχίαις ἀποστροφὴν ἐκ ἀπολείπεσιν—with much more to the same purpose. The whole of it is perhaps one of the finest passages in Plutarch's writings.

viz.

viz. that happiness is *actually* prepollent in this system. This, as has been already observed, is a subject of difficult investigation. We can only *judge* of those parts which are known to us, and *conjecture* of those which are unknown.

1. Then let each man consider *himself.*—Does he not think life a benefit? Would he not think the loss of it a misfortune? Are not his pleasures more frequent, tho' less attended to, than his pains? Are not the deep impressions, made by these, to be imputed more to the rarity, than the degree, of them? Does he not pass a considerable part of *every* day in a manner which gives him *some* pleasure? Are not *those* days comparatively *few*, in which he has found any considerable degree of *bodily* pain? Is not his uneasiness of *mind* less frequent and permanent, than his chearfulness and satisfaction?

To these questions, no doubt, different answers will be given by different men. But he who answers them all in the affirmative, has at least *one* good argument, and in which he cannot well be deceived, for admitting the doctrine of *prepollent good.*

2. Let

2. Let each man conjecture, as well as he can, concerning the happiness of his *friends* and *acquaintance*, and of all those who come under his *immediate* notice.—Possibly he will find many of them furnished with various means of pleasure; few of them subject to great misfortunes: many more healthy than sick; many more, competently provided with the conveniences of life, than struggling with want and difficulties; many more, possessed of friends and relations, whom they love and who love them, than oppressed and persecuted by enemies; many more, happy in the hope of future good, than alarmed by the fear of impending evil.—He who finds this to be a true representation, will be still more strongly inclined to admit the *prepollency* of good in our present system.

It must not be thought an objection to this conclusion, that many more are *poor*, than *rich*. For we only give the name of *rich* to those who are *peculiarly* so: as of* beautiful, wise, strong, tall, to those who are *above* the

---

* So Balbus in Cic. de Nat. Deorum, lib. 2. c. 28. Motus enim quisque *formosus* est ? Athenis cum essem, è gregibus Epheborum vix singuli reperiebantur.

common

common rate. It will be enough to satisfy an impartial inquirer, if he finds many more in *plenty*, than in *want* : i. e. able to provide what their station in life requires, and *not unhappy* from the desire of a higher station *.

3. Let each man examine the most authentic accounts of *distant* times and places. Possibly he will see cause to conjecture, that the persons *unknown* to him have not, in general, been less happy, than those he knows. If, in other ages and nations, the circumstances of mankind appear not so favourable as in ours; it is probable, however, that the wants and the tempers of men are every where *accommodated* to their circumstances, at least in a considerable degree; and that others may even be *happy* in those situations, in which *we* should think ourselves exquisitely miserable †.

Thus

---

* Seneca goes farther (Conf. ad Helv. c. 12.) Aspice, quanto major sit pars pauperum, quos nihilo notabis tristiores, sollicitioresque divisibus: imo nescio an eo *lætiores* sint, quo animus eorum in pauciora distringitur.

† Nullum invenies exilium, in quo non aliquis *animi causâ* moretur. Sen. ad Helvid. c. 6.

And

Thus the inhabitants of some parts of *Africa* might appear to *us* to be in the lowest and most wretched state; as wanting almost every advantage of social life. No *arts, learning, laws*: and, of course, a very precarious enjoyment of their lives and possessions. Yet it has been found, that these very men, when removed to England, have regretted the loss of their own country, and expressed the utmost impatience to return to it. Which could not possibly have been the case, if they had not, on the *whole*, been *pleased* with their former situation.

If this appears to be a *just* view of the state of mankind, it must be owned, that the present system of things produces *prepollent* good. If it be controverted, the objections will probably fall under one or other of the following heads *.

And again——
Nihil miserum est, quod in naturam confuetudo perduxit. Paullatim enim voluptati sunt, quæ necessitate cœperunt. Nulla illis domicilia (he speaks of the Germans) nullæ sedes sunt; nisi quas lassitudo in diem posuit; vilis, et hic quærendus manu, victus; horrenda iniquitas cœli; intecta corpora: hoc quod tibi calamitas videtur, tot gentium vita est. Sen. de Prov. c. 4.

* These objections are taken from a beautiful declamation of *Wollaston's*, in the 9th sect. of his Religion of Nature delineated.

1. That,

1. That, even in *peaceful* and settled times, the pains of life exceed the pleasures.—Or, if this be given up,

2. That the calamities of *war* are fatal to the repose and happiness of the world; and that these calamities are so frequent, as to involve a very confiderable part of the human species. Or

3. That many innocent perfons are rendered unhappy by *tyranny* and *perfecution*.---To which may be added,

4. That the *evils* of human life conftitute the chief objects of *hiftory*; and that this clearly shews the prefent world to be a ftate of misery, not of happiness.

I.

It is alledged, that, even in peaceful and fettled times, the pains men fuffer exceed their pleafures. For that

1. They who are moft fuccefsful, have many cares and troubles, little fincere pleafure: and

2. Numbers of men are altogether unfuccefsful.

1. They

1. They who are succefsful in life have many cares and troubles, which are very sensibly felt: and they have little sincere pleasure to balance these feelings.—*Childhood*, we are told, suffers much uneasiness from the restraint and discipline, to which it is subject; and receives no pleasures in return, but such as are trifling and vain.—*Manhood* is exposed to inconveniences in the transaction of *business*, from the negligence, perverseness, or knavery, of those with whom we deal; to *domestic* disquiets, from the faults of our wives, or children, or servants; and to frequent vexation, from the unkindness, or misbehaviour, even of our common acquaintance and neighbours. Its enjoyments, on the other hand, are deceitful; mixed with uneasiness; difficult also to be attained, as usually requiring the concurrence of a variety of circumstances; and, lastly, of short duration, soon lost and forgotten, as if they had never been.—*Old age* is subject to still greater difficulties, and has less ability to struggle with them. The loss of our friends and relations, the pains and sickness we must usually expect

in that period of life, are surely very trying circumstances.

To all this may be added a general remark, which is thought a full confirmation of the description here given ; viz. that the most *fortunate* of men would not wish a *repetition* of their past lives.

In answer to this objection, it may be said more truly, that the *sufferings* of childhood are trifling, the pleasures great.—We only esteem them insignificant, because they are not suited to the taste of mature age. It is enough, that they suit the capacity and inclination of those who enjoy them : and they are far from being balanced, nay they are recommended and improved, by intervals of restraint. In this period of our lives, as in every other, our time is divided between amusement and business : the constant returns of which makes both more agreeable. In short, the happiness of children is apparent, to whatever cause we may impute it, from their perpetual chearfulness and fulness of spirits.

The common cares of *manhood* hold no proportion with its satisfactions. It may safely

safely be affirmed, that, in all ordinary cases, the pleasure arising from our *domestic* affections far exceeds the anxiety which attends them: and, in many instances too, the anxiety itself is mixed with pleasure. Misbehaviour in the persons, with whom we have an intercourse of *business*, occasions indeed inconvenience and disappointment. But these things give little disturbance to a man who is *accustomed* to expect them; and often occasion *pleasure*, by giving room for our skill and prudence, in guarding against them. For, without opposition, there could be no victory. As for *quarrels* with our acquaintance and neighbours; they cannot be a very considerable mischief. For no man, I suppose, to avoid this evil, would wish to pass his days in solitude. On the other hand, the *enjoyments* of this state are various: some of them permanent; others transient indeed, but anticipated by hope, or delightful even on reflection.—If the objects of our wishes are found not answerable to our expectations, this destroys not our happiness. For *new* wishes are formed; and new pleasures received from every step we take towards their gratification.

If the enjoyments themselves are not what they seem; yet the very *hope* of obtaining them is a constant source of happiness.

For the comforts and pleasures of *old age,* see *Cicero de Senectute,* where the subject is indeed exhausted.

The fallacy of the *general* remark is very obvious. Whatever pleasures we may have enjoyed in our past lives, we expect *no* pleasure from the repetition. Novelty and variety either are, or seem to be, *essential* to our happiness: and hence it comes to pass, that the frequent returns of the *same* enjoyments appear, in imagination, flat and insipid. But no conclusion can be drawn from this appearance; which in truth is nothing more than an illusion of the fancy. Add to this, that the ills of life are perhaps better *remembered* than the goods. The former affect us more forcibly, because they are less frequent: the latter, being familiar and common, make no deep impression on the mind. On *both* accounts we deceive ourselves in the judgments we form of our past lives.

Thus far, however, we have only seen the condition of mankind in its fairest light: we have

have only attended to that part of our species who are *succefsful* in the world. But

2. Numbers of men are altogether *unfuccefsful*. They never obtain a comfortable settlement, or they are afterwards deprived of it. They are unhappy in the mifbehaviour of their families and friends, or in the lofs of them. Their wifeft fchemes are defeated by untoward accidents: and they languifh under misfortunes, of mind, or body, or fortune, which no care or caution was capable of preventing. Thefe cafes, indeed, are fo frequent, and fo ftriking, that they are become the daily fubject of converfation: every hour almoft prefents us with fome new fcene of want or mifery; and objects of diftrefs are continually before our eyes.

To this may be anfwered, that the picture is not fairly drawn. It is heightened beyond probability and nature.

In times of peace (for of fuch only are we fpeaking) the far *greater* part of mankind both obtain and preferve a competent fhare of the neceffaries and conveniences of life. Many of thofe who do not, fuffer lefs than is imagined; and many acquire by habit an

ability

ability to bear their misfortunes. Others meet with unexpected relief and comfort: others end their cares and their lives together.

The *misbehaviour* of families and friends, tho' a severe affliction to *some* dispositions, is not so to *all:* with many it is not of force enough to destroy their chearfulness and happiness. *Small* faults in those we love deprive us not of the pleasure we receive from them: *great* faults destroy the affection we bear them, and leave us unconcerned spectators of what they do or suffer. The affliction we feel on the *loss* of our near relations, is a proof of the great pleasure we once received from them: and the pleasure was *permanent*; the grief soon passes away.

Nor is it to be wondered, that we see and hear so much of the evils of life. Among the vast numbers of the human species, there may be frequent accidents and calamities; yet *many more*, who escape, than who suffer them. If they were more common, they would be less remarked. They are frequently made subjects of conversation; because men are curious to hear of singular events,

and

and take a pleasure in indulging their compassion.

II.

Whatever may be said of peaceful times, *war*, we are told, and the *consequences* of war, are fatal to multitudes. Many are deprived of all the comforts of life: many more of life itself; not those only who fall in the field, but those who are exposed, by military plunder, to nakedness and hunger, and perish for want of the necessary means of preservation. Nor are these calamities rare in the world, and extraordinary. [Unhappily, they are so frequent, as to involve a great part of the human species.

In abatement, however, of this accumulated charge, several considerations may be offered.

1st. The *lives* lost in war are foreign to the purpose. For it ought not to be considered as a diminution of a man's happiness, that his life is ended by a *musquet*, rather than a *fever*.

2dly. The *dangers* attending a state of war become, from habit, so familiar, that the persons exposed to them feel little uneasiness.

3dly. The *poverty*, and perhaps *slavery*, which follow, may indeed in *some* men produce great affliction; but not in the *generality*. These evils are only felt by men who know what it is to be *rich* and *free*. The rest suffer no great change. They always have been, and they continue to be, subject to *labour*; and receive, in return for it, a competent share, sometimes a plentiful share, of the conveniences of life.—*Slavery* was, in ancient times, the lot of every prisoner of war: and must have extended therefore to great numbers of men. But the condition of slaves is usually much less miserable, than we are apt to imagine. They may suffer, no doubt, and too often do suffer, from the cruelty of their *master*. But it is his *interest* to use them well: and *most* men, we may suppose, understand their interest, and pursue it. Even in this land of liberty, men have sometimes been found, who wished us to follow the *example* of the ancients; and maintained that

that the inftitution of *domeftic flavery* was beneficial to the world *.

4thly. It fhould not be quite forgotten, that, while the condition of fome men is rendered worfe by war, that of others is rendered *better*.

Indeed, the *whole* number, made unhappy by thefe public calamities, bears no proportion to the bulk of mankind. In nations totally reduced by conqueft, it has fometimes happened, that a very confiderable part of the inhabitants have been reduced to fervitude. But thefe inftances are rare. Very few occur in our own times; and we may reafonably hope, that the practice of antiquity, notwithftanding it has met with fome able advocates, will never again revive among civilized nations.

---

* It appears from innumerable inftances, that flaves, among the Greeks and Romans, lived in a very different manner from *modern* flaves. Judge from the following paffage of Seneca, de Prov. c. 1.———Cum videris bonos viros, acceptofque Diis, laborare, fudare, per arduum afcendere, malos autem *lafcivire et voluptatibus fluere*, cogita filiorum nos modeftiâ delectari, *vernularum licentiâ*.

III.

It is said, that many innocent persons are rendered unhappy by *tyranny* and *persecution*. But

1st. The effects of *tyranny* are usually confined to a *few* persons; seldom extend, unless indirectly, to the *body* of a people. Even under the government of such wretches as *Nero* and *Domitian*, many thousands of men, thro' all parts of the empire, lived in plenty, and quiet, and security*. Nay, the distant provinces were perhaps *more* secure, than when exposed to the plunder of republican governors. With regard to the few, who become objects of envy, or jealousy, or resentment, they must, of course, fall victims to absolute power. But that power is more frequently exerted in *shortening* men's lives, than in making them *miserable* while they live.

2dly. *Persecution* is indeed confined to no rank of men. No age or sex escapes its fury.

---

* See in Plut. περὶ ἐυθυμίας, a description of the general happiness men enjoyed, I know not under what prince, but certainly under a despotic government.—Διε δὲ κỳ τὰ κοινὰ, &c.

But

But then it is ufually of fhort continuance: for either the objects of it are deftroyed, or, by collecting themfelves into numbers, and making a vigorous refiftance, they are able to fhake off the yoke which oppreffes them. The perfecution indeed of the primitive Chriftians, even when freed from the rubbifh of uncertain traditions, and divefted of every circumftance, which folly or fraud has annexed to it, will ftill furnifh fomething like an exception to this remark. Yet the numbers, we know, of thofe who fuffered, have been great'y magnified: the intervals of quiet, which the church enjoyed, were very frequent, and fometimes long; and very feldom did the mifchief prevail at once through all the parts of the Roman empire. The fufferers, no doubt, were many of them put to death in a way more painful than the common lot of humanity. But in thefe pains they were wonderfully fupported: perhaps by a divine fpirit; certainly by the profpect of a happy immortality: which was believed by them with a degree of affurance and confidence, that, in a manner, *counteracted* their natural feelings,

feelings, and enabled them to *rejoice* under the severest tortures.

The singularity of this case has led me out of the way. But I shall now return; and shall briefly consider the fourth head of objection already mentioned.

IV.

The objector concludes, that this world is a place of misery, because the chief objects of *history*, in every age, have been the *calamities* of mankind.—But there is very little force in this objection. For

1st. History describes the *changes* only in public affairs; not the continuance of peaceful government, and the happy influence of it. These, from their very nature, can have little room in an historical narration; tho' they may do well enough for a panegyrical declaimer. For it is clearly impossible, that a writer should collect and describe the various enjoyments of particular families, living under equal laws. They are not known to him: they seldom, if ever, become public. Whereas the oppressions of *magistrates*; the tumults of
subjects,

subjects; *war, famine, pestilence*; are open to general observation.

2dly. If such events *could* be known, they would not be *related.* For the historian is chiefly employed about the transaction of *governors*, and no farther considers private persons than as acting *under* them, or *against* them. He describes, therefore, the *mischiefs* which men suffer, either from the *abuse* of power, or the *resistance* made to it; from the *wars* in which they engage, or which they are obliged to *repel*; and from every instance of civil or of foreign *dissension*. But the *good* derived from a regular administration of justice is passed over; as the supreme magistrate does not immediately appear in it.

3dly. Historians are most apt to enlarge on such events as will be most *affecting* to their readers. They know the strength of compassion; and they know, how *pleasing* it is to the human mind. They therefore *designedly* expatiate on scenes of distress, because they are sure men will delight in the representation.

4thly. If the observation have any force at all, it rather lies on the *contrary* side. For, since

since historians are chiefly employed in describing the *evils* of life; it looks, as if they thought these more remarkable than the goods: and this again is a presumption, that they are less *common*.—Just as, in a history of the heavens, an astronomer would not relate, day by day, the customary changes of *light* and *darkness:* but would enumerate *eclipses* or *comets*, or any other unusual phænomena.

But, beside what has been said, in answer to *each* of *Wollaston's* objections, they are *all* liable to one very obvious answer, viz. that he has only attended to *one side* of the question. He has dwelt largely on the melancholy parts of human life; but, in a great measure, overlooked its enjoyments. A pen like his could, with equal ease and success, have painted the *happiness* of our present state, and given it the appearance of a *paradise.*— But to form a *true* estimate, we must set one thing against another; and afterwards pronounce, if we can, on which side the balance turns.——In the mean time we may discern, on the first face of things, that the

Author

Author of Nature is *not malevolent* *; and that therefore we have *nothing* to oppose, from *fact* and *experience*, against the various proofs of kind *intention*, which were alledged in the first part of this treatise. Probably, indeed, an impartial inquirer will go farther than this: and will appeal to experience for a full and final *confirmation* of the doctrine of DIVINE BENEVOLENCE.

* What might be expected from a being of *that* character, is pointed out, p. 180 of *Hutcheson on the Passions*.—See also, in the same book, p. 182, a comparative view of our pleasures and pains.

APPENDIX.

Containing a short Theory of the Passions.

THIS is a subject, on which different writers, if they are attentive to what passes within their own minds, will unavoidably coincide. Such is the uniformity of our nature, that very nearly the same observations will occur to all thinking men. I shall not scruple therefore to repeat what has been said by others; or even to use their expressions, when they suit my purpose.

Previous Remarks.

1. The *image* of pleasure pleases: the image of pain displeases.
2. An *opinion* entertained that the pleasure will actually be enjoyed, or the pain suffered,

gives

gives a much *higher* pleasure or pain, than the bare imagination of either.

On the other hand, an opinion entertained, that we shall *not* enjoy the pleasure, or *not* suffer the pain, causes the agreeable image to become painful, and the disagreeable image to become pleasing.——In other words thus—The efficacy of any object in producing pleasure will give us pain, when we despair of obtaining it : and the efficacy of any object in causing pain, will give us pleasure, when we are assured of our own security.

3. The *customary causes* of pleasure and pain usually please or displease, when they become objects of imagination; the idea of the effect being *associated* with the idea of the cause : and, of course, those qualities in the object, whether animate or inanimate, on which that effect depends, become agreeable or disagreeable in imagination.

The power we have of feeling *present* pleasure or pain from reflecting on what will be, or may be, hereafter, we shall call *anticipation*.

APPENDIX.

4. The effects resulting from this power of anticipation are much altered by *comparison*: which

1st, Magnifies the larger, and diminishes the less, of the goods, or ills, compared;

2dly, Increases the pleasure or pain, when the *magnified* object is *expected*;

3dly, Causes us to feel pain, from the objects which naturally please, and pleasure from those which naturally displease, when the *diminished* object is expected.——In other words,

A cause of pleasure or pain, when compared with a more powerful one, will produce less effect, or none at all, or even a *contrary* effect.

5. The thoughts and feelings of *others*, as soon as they are made known or imagined, excite *similar* perceptions in us, provided no contrary cause interfere. This is called *sympathy*. But these perceptions, as well as others, are liable to be interrupted, or inverted, by the influence of *comparison*; and are often too overpowered by the superior force of those sentiments which regard *ourselves*.

It may appear perhaps, on inquiry, that all our paffions are derived from one or more of thefe principles: viz. Imagination, opinion, affociation, comparifon, fympathy. The three firft we comprehend under the general name of anticipation.

Let us now proceed to a particular examination of each paffion.

1ft. We have already obferved, that the pleafures or pains we feel from imagination are increafed by opinion: and we may add too, that they increafe in proportion to the *degree* of affurance, with which the event is expected.—Suppofe now two *contrary* events to be either imagined or apprehended, and that we know not which of them will take place; in this cafe there will evidently be a *mixture* of pleafure and pain: and either of thefe may prevail, in any affignable degree, in proportion to the degrees of doubt and affurance.

When our expectations of good or evil are in this *uncertain* fituation, the paffions excited are called *defire* and *averfion*: when *certain*, they are called *joy* and *forrow*.

As

As the expectation of good or ill success appears more or less *probable*, desire and aversion take the names of *hope* and *fear*.

2dly. In each man's imagination, the *power* of enjoying pleasure, implies the *certain* enjoyment of it. Hence the *acquisition* of this power pleases; and the prospect, or image, of such acquisition also pleases. The *power* therefore of enjoying, as well as the *actual* enjoyment, becomes an object of desire.

From this source we derive the desires of *liberty, dominion, property*. *Fame* too, as it gives some degree of power, must also become an object of desire.

3dly. If by any means we should come to participate the pleasures and pains of others, *their* enjoyments also, and the means of obtaining them, would, in like manner, become objects of desire.

4thly. If by any means we should come to receive pain from the pleasures of others, and pleasure from their pains; *their* enjoyments, and the means of enjoying them, would become objects of aversion.

5thly. Besides a variety of subordinate desires, comprehended under these heads, the

general

general idea of happiness, whether selfish or social, constitutes a superior object of desire, distinct from each particular pleasure, and *v.v.* and there are also cases, in which it may constitute a destinct object of aversion. But the passions excited by general causes are usually more feeble than those which aim-at particular objects.

The passions hitherto described arise from reflecting either on the *sensations* themselves, whether pleasant or painful; or on the *events* which may produce, or give occasion to, them. But the various *objects* also, animate or inanimate, which are capable of *causing* pleasure or pain, will become agreeable or disagreeable on reflection. Hence we derive the passions of *esteem* and *disesteem*; *benevolence* and *malevolence*; the sense of *honour*, and the *moral* sense.

1. *Of esteem and disesteem.*

1. We esteem *ourselves* for actions or qualities, which either produce *immediate* pleasure, or increase the *power* of pleasing, or the *will* to please; and we usually take into our view the pleasure

pleasure of *others* as well as our own. Even the *external* circumstances, in which we are placed, give rise to like sentiments, when they are thought capable of producing like effects. A man esteems himself for his *wealth*, as well as for his wisdom.—On the other hand, the power of giving *pain* to others, if that pain have become an object of desire, is equally capable of producing self-esteem.

2. We *disesteem* ourselves for any observable *deficiency* in such qualities, or for any actions or qualities, which *disable* us from doing good or harm, or which may probably be the *occasions* of doing or suffering harm.

3. In like manner we are led to esteem *others* from observing in them either agreeable or useful qualities, and to *disesteem* them from observing either a *want* of these, or an appearance of *opposite* qualities, viz. such as make them less able, or less willing, to please.

The esteem and disesteem of others is of two kinds. Qualities, which cause good only, excite *love*; qualities, which cause ill only, excite *hatred*. Those which increase the *power*, without determining the *application*, give rise to *respect*: the opposite defects and qualities provoke *contempt*.

1. Since *love* arises towards those, in whom we discern agreeable or useful qualities, we can be at no loss to account for the different *kinds* of love. The love of our *acquaintance* proceeds from *frequent* pleasure received; the love of *benefactors* (or gratitude) from *great* advantages conferred: and, since it is natural to be pleased with the regards of others, we readily make returns of love to those who love *us*. The love of the *sexes* is *founded* on sensual pleasures; but *increased* by those we receive from beauty, wit, or any other accomplishment. The love of our *offspring* depends on the same principles. Nature indeed seems to have rendered our children pleasing to us *antecedently* to any agreeable or useful qualities, they may happen to possess; which however are sure not to escape the eye of a parent. This perhaps proceeds from the regard we have to *ourselves*; which, by the power of association, is readily extended to every thing related to us. Doubtless the sentiment is very much heightened by the pleasures

pleasures our children *actually* give us, and the many more we *expect* to receive from them.

The occasions of *hatred* are easily understood from what has been said of its opposite. All qualities give birth to this passion, which are causes of *pain* : and as nothing is more painful than *contempt*, every appearance of this sentiment is sure to provoke resentment. Whence some writers have represented such appearances as the *only* source of of our malignant passions *. But this is a fanciful supposition, and unsupported by experience.—There is besides *another* species of hatred, arising from *competition*: in which the phænomena are in a manner *inverted* ; and hatred arises from the customary causes of respect and love.

To prevent mistakes on this subject, it may be fit to observe, that even *inanimate* causes of pleasure, as they cannot but please in imagination, are often said to produce *love*; and *v. v.* But though the same word be used, the sentiment is very distinguishable. When we speak of loving *grapes*, or hating

* Arist. Rhet. lib. 2.

phyfic, our meaning is not the fame, as when we fpeak of loving our *children*, or hating a *tyrant*.

2. *Respect* arifes from qualities or circumftances capable of being applied either to good or ill. This fentiment feldom rifes high, unlefs we difcern a remarkable difparity between others and ourfelves. Hence often proceeds an uneafy reflection, which is apt to terminate in hatred.

Contempt arifes from obferving either a remarkable deficiency in fuch qualities, or an appearance of other qualities inconfiftent with them.

Before we quit this part of the fubject, it fhould be obferved, that the efteem a man obtains from others confirms him in the good opinion he had of himfelf; and therefore cannot fail of being acceptable to him. His felf-efteem too is farther increafed by fympathy: and, on both accounts, *fame* (already an object of defire, for the reafon before given) is rendered ftill more defirable.

II. *Of benevolence and malevolence.*

1. Benevolence is only a fpecies of *fympathy.*—*General* benevolence is a principle of
little

little force*, unless when the imagination is strongly impressed with the *pains* of others; in which case it takes the name of *compassion*.—Benevolence to *particular* persons constantly attends *love*, of whatever kind, and, where there is no competition, is sometimes also produced by *respect*.

2. *General* malevolence is a principle seldom, if ever, to be found in our nature.— Malevolence to particular persons usually results from the opinion we entertain of their characters and conduct. For this opinion, as we have seen, produces *hatred:* and hatred seldom exists, without some degree of ill-will. *Anger* may be considered as a species of hatred; arising (for the most part) from some apparent injury, and producing a strong, but temporary, *malevolence*.—Malevolence, when independent on personal character, results from *comparison*. We *envy* in others the goods we want, whether of nature or fortune: and we sometimes feel a *malicious* pleasure, in surveying those evils, from which we ourselves are free †.

* This is to be understood of its *immediate* influence : for *indirectly*, as it gives occasion to *moral* sentiments, it may have very considerable effect.

† The Greeks had a name for this principle as well as it's opposite. Φθόνος μὲν γάρ ἐστι λύπη ἐπ' ἀλλοτρίοις ἀγαθοῖς, ἐπιχαιρεκακία δὲ ἡδονὴ ἐπ' ἀλλοτρίοις κακοῖς. Plut. de Curios.

III. *Of*

III. *Of the Sense of Honour.*

This sentiment has been incidentally explained already: I only give it a place here, in conformity to the practice of other writers; for it is evidently included in the passions mentioned above. We have but to repeat, and unite, the considerations before suggested.

We receive pleasure from the *belief*, or *imagination*, that we possess the esteem of others, on two accounts: 1. Because the good opinion of others confirms the opinion we have of ourselves; and the esteem of others, by the force of *sympathy*, strengthens our self-esteem: 2. Because the principle of *association* has connected the esteem of others with the *advantages* to be obtained from their friendship. The truth of this account will be seen by observing, *whose* esteem it is that we value most: viz, their's, whose *opinion* has most weight, or whose *friendship* is supposed to be most useful.

On the other hand, we receive *pain* from the *contempt* or *dislike* of others, as depriving us of both these advantages.—To this head belongs

belongs the paffion of *fhame*: which is only a difefteem of ourfelves, joined to a quick fenfe of honour. The fame fenfe of honour, when joined with *felf-efteem*, takes the name of *vanity*. In the one cafe we are anxious to avoid *difgrace*, in the other to obtain *applaufe*.

IV. *Of the Moral Senfe.*

There is one kind of fentiment ftill to be added, which was defigned for the regulation of all the reft, *approbation* and *difapprobation*. The power of receiving thefe fentiments is called by fome the *moral fenfe*: by others, who feem to have thought the word *fenfe* might be liable to a wrong interpretation, the *moral faculty*.—Call it what you pleafe, there are certain *feelings* in the mind, the objects of which, and indeed the *peculiar* objects, are determinations of the *will*. Voluntary obedience to any ufeful principle of action, or voluntary refiftance to any hurtful principle, produces approbation; the contrary, difapprobation *: perhaps from our
anticipating

---

* It may be objected perhaps that *all* the principles in our nature may be fhewn to be ufeful. They are fo when not *abufed*,

anticipating the good or ill which ufually arife from fuch conduct, and *fympathizing* with thofe, who are fuppofed to enjoy the one, or fuffer the other.—It is difficult to conceive, how it can have happened, that the *reality* of thefe fentiments fhould ever have been difputed. They are not indeed *innate:* for *no* fentiments are innate. But they are *common*, I fuppofe, to our whole fpecies. There is not a nation upon earth, whofe language wants words to exprefs thefe feelings: probably there never was a fingle man, who was void of all perception of *right* and *wrong*.

The fentiment above-defcribed is diftinguifhable from all others, not only by our inward confcioufnefs, but by the following *marks* which are infeparable from it. It does not depend on the *fuccefs* of men's endeavours; but fimply on the *intention* with which they act. It has no peculiar relation to *ourfelves*; but rather gives a *preference* to

abufed, i. e. mifapplied, or exceffive. They are fo, in their proper *place*, i. e. not interfering with more extenfive, or more important principles of action. In either of thefe cafes, a good principle changes it's name and it's nature: and is no longer intitled to our regard and compliance.

other men, and principally regards the *general* happiness. It is constantly attended with another sense, which may almost be considered as a part of it; the sense of good and ill *desert*. Whoever *rewards* the man we approve, or *punishes* the man we disapprove, becomes *himself* on that account an object of approbation.

Observe however that the moral sentiment, as well as every other, may not only be produced by it's own *peculiar* cause, but also by *sympathy*: and thus, in fact, it seems to be *first* introduced into every human mind.

Before we conclude this subject, it may be fit to take notice, that this sense or faculty is not usually numbered among the *passions*. Nay, on the contrary, it assumes very frequently the name of *reason*. Language is arbitrary, and therefore various. I can only say, that these *moral* feelings are, as much as any *other*, *modes of pleasure and pain*, though perhaps less violent than the rest. If you dislike the words *sense* and *passion*, use any other, that will express the same *idea*; and it will serve the purpose equally well.

That

That we like or dislike beneficial or hurtful *actions*; that these sentiments lead us to like or dislike the *agents*, if acting with design and choice; and that these agents are finally *approved* or *disapproved*, as acting under the influence of good or bad *principles*: these only are the material points, which we mean to assert.

Recapitulation.

1. Some passions respect indifferently good and evil of all kinds, and all the various objects, which are capable of producing or preventing either.—Such are our desires and aversions; hopes and fears; joys and sorrows.

2. Other passions respect only *intelligent* causes of pleasure or pain. Such are esteem and disesteem; benevolence and malevolence; the sense of honour and dishonour; the sense of moral good and evil.

3. All these passions are founded on this principle, that the image of pleasure pleases, the image of pain displeases. They are drawn

drawn from this source, in various ways, by anticipation, comparison, and sympathy.

4. These observations are applicable not only to other passions, but to the moral faculty itself: which may be considered as a *peculiar* species of esteem and disesteem, confined to the determinations of the *will*.

END OF THE APPENDIX.

(145)

Printed for LOCKYER DAVIS.

I. ON CHURCH GOVERNMENT. A Sermon, preached at the Confecration of the Right Rev. Jonathan Shipley, D. D. Lord Bifhop of Landaff, Feb. 12, 1769.

II. ON THE RESPECTIVE DUTIES OF MINISTERS AND PEOPLE. A Sermon, preached at Lambeth Chapel, at the Confecration of the Right Rev. Richard Hurd, D. D. Lord Bifhop of Lichfield and Coventry; and of the Right Rev. John Moore, D. D. Lord Bifhop of Bangor. The above by Thomas Balguy, D. D. Archdeacon of Winchefter.

III. A Charge delivered to the Clergy of the Archdeaconry of Winchefter, in the Year 1772.

" To propofe the *Amendment* of fome particulars in the prefent eftablifhment, in order to the making it more perfect, is what cannot well be complained of. But to propofe a fcheme, which cannot be admitted without the entire *deftruction* and total *abolition* of the whole prefent conftitution, can end in no good."

HOADLY.

IV. Difcourfes on Various Subjects. By William Samuel Powell, D. D. Late Archdeacon of Colchefter, and Mafter of St. John's College, Cambridge. Publifhed by Thomas Balguy, D. D. price 5s.

V. A Key to the New Teftament. Giving an Account of the feveral Books, their Contents, their Authors, and the Times, Places and Occafions on which they were refpectively written.

By the Rev. Dr. Thomas Percy, D. D. Dean of Carlifle. The fecond Edition, revifed and improved. 2s. 6d.

VI. Bifhop Sherlock's Difcourfes: the *Fifth* and laft Volume.

N. B. This Volume confifts of Fourteen Difcourfes, preached on important occafions; being all that were separately

separately published by his Lordship now first collected. Price 5s.

VII. Bishop Atterbury's Sermons, 4 Vols.

VIII. Dr. Brown's Sermons on various Subjects, 5s.

IX. Dr. Brown's Essays on Lord Shaftsbury's Characteristics. Fourth Edition, 5s.

X. Dr. Bundy's Sermons, 3 Vols. or the *Third Volume* separate, 5s.

XI. Archbishop Sharpe's Sermons, 7 Vols. *in Twelves*.

XII. The Passion: or Descriptive and Critical Narrative of the interesting and important Events as they occurred on each Day of the Week, in which Christ's Sufferings are commemorated. In which the Harmony of the Four Evangelists is settled: and to each Narrative are subjoined Reflexions calculated for Religious Improvement. By Thomas Knowles, D.D. Prebendary of Ely, 3s.

This day are published, an accurate Edition in French and another in English, price 2s. 6d.

The REVOLUTION of AMERICA. By the Abbé Raynal, Author of the Philosophical and Political History of both the Indies.

In the above Piece, which comprehends a circumstantial Detail of the Disputes between Great-Britain and her Colonies, the illustrious Historian, in his zeal for the Rights of Mankind, points out the proper means for healing the distressful Breach, and restoring this Empire to her pristine Glory.

www.ingramcontent.com/pod-product-compliance
Lightning Source LLC
Chambersburg PA
CBHW030320170426
43202CB00009B/1083